THE LIFE AND TIMES OF EMMA GOLDMAN

A Curriculum for Middle and High School Students

Primary Historical Documents on:

Immigration
Freedom of Expression
Women's Rights
Anti-Militarism
Art and Literature of Social Change

Prepared by the Emma Goldman Papers Project
University of California, Berkeley
in association with New Directions Curriculum Developers
and the Los Angeles Educational Partnership

APPLIES STANDARD SOCIAL STUDIES
AND HUMANITIES CURRICULUM
THEMES

The Life and Times of Emma Goldman

A Curriculum for Middle and High School Students

Primary Historical Documents on:
Immigration
Freedom of Expression
Women's Rights
Anti-Militarism
Art and Literature of Social Change

Second Edition

The Emma Goldman Papers
University of California, Berkeley

The Emma Goldman Papers Project
University of California
2372 Ellsworth Street
Berkeley, CA 94720

For educational purposes, the editors have added illustrations to original texts, and produced facsimile documents for legibility and readability. Every effort has been made to match the appearance of the original documents.

Second edition December 1992

Library of Congress Cataloging-in-Publication Data
The Life and times of Emma Goldman: a curriculum for middle and high school students: primary historical documents/principal writers, Candace Falk, Lyn Reese and Mary Agnes Dougherty.
p. cm.
Includes bibliographical references.
ISBN 0-9635443-0-6: $13.00
1. Goldman, Emma, 1869-1940—Biography—Sources. 2. Anarchism—History—Sources. 3. Women's rights—History—Sources. 4. Militarism—History—Sources. 5. Literature and society—History—Sources. I. Falk, Candace. II. Reese, Lyn, 1938- III. Dougherty, Mary Agnes.
HX843.7.G65L53 1992
335'.83'092—dc20
[B] 92-45687
CIP

Additional copies of this curriculum are available for $13.00 plus $3.00 shipping/handling; make checks out to "UC Regents/Emma Goldman Papers." (California residents: please add 7.25% sales tax). For more information call: 510-643-8518.

Principal Writers
Candace Falk, Ph.D.
Lyn Reese and Mary Agnes Dougherty

Editors and Production Staff
Managing Editors: Sally Thomas and Stephen Cole, Ph.D.
Susan Wengraf

Research Assistants
Tamara Falicov
Allyson Roessler
Amy Scharf

Los Angeles Educational Partnership Advisors
Neil Anstead
James Bechtel
Alexa Maxwell
Chris Miller
Eric Schoenbaum
Patrick Scott
Howard Wilf

Consultants
June Brumer
Sarah Crome
Elise Trumbull Estrin
Susan Groves
Sheila Weintraub
Beth Wilson

This publication was made possible by a grant from the Los Angeles Educational Partnership.

New Directions Curriculum Developers specializes in creating educational materials for schools, museums, videos, and special projects. For more information, contact:
Lyn Reese and Mary Agnes Dougherty
1030 Spruce Street
Berkeley, CA 94707
510-524-0304

The modern school, in teaching history, must bring before the child a panorama of dramatic periods and incidents, illustrative of the main movements and epochs of human development. It must, therefore, help to develop an appreciation in the child of the struggle of past generations, for progress and liberty, and thereby develop a respect for every truth that aims to emancipate the human race.... A new day is dawning when the school will serve life in all its phases and reverently lift each human child to its appropriate place in a common life of beneficent social efficiency, whose motto will be not uniformity and discipline but freedom, expansion, good will and joy for each and all.

—Emma Goldman, "The Social Importance of the Modern School" (Emma Goldman Papers, Rare Books and Manuscripts Division, New York Public Library).

Table of Contents

Table of Contents, continued

Preface: Linking Emma Goldman to Standard Curriculum Themes

Emma Goldman (1869-1940) is a major figure in the history of American radicalism and feminism. In a period when the expression of controversial ideas was itself dangerous, Goldman insisted on her right to challenge convention. Goldman devoted her life to asserting the individual's potential for freedom that otherwise was obscured by a system of social and economic constraints. She was among America's most prominent advocates of labor's right to organize, reproductive rights, sexual freedom, freedom of speech, and freedom of the individual.

As passionate in her personal life as in her political life, Goldman left an intriguing body of personal papers, including correspondence and writings; and her activities generated extensive newspaper coverage, government surveillance reports, and legal papers. The documents in this curriculum unit are drawn from a massive archive collected by the Emma Goldman Papers Project. They are linked to the following standard social studies and humanities curriculum themes:

Art and literature—Social change reflected through creative expression

First Amendment rights—Legislative restraints against individual expression and privacy, free speech campaigns, free speech organizations, vigilante violence, legal challenges defining the right to dissent, analysis of federal vs. state and local authorities' jurisdiction over First Amendment rights

Labor—Factory conditions, labor unrest, violence against strikers, the Industrial Workers of the World, syndicalism, organizing for the eight-hour work day

Progressive Politics—Definition and appeal of anarchism, McKinley assassination, similarities and differences between reformers, socialists, anarchists, communists, and liberal progressives

Red Scare—Government investigation of radicals and raids of their offices and organizations, arrests and deportation, particular vulnerability of aliens to political repression

Rise of industrialism—Conditions of industrial workers, workers in conflict with industrial capitalists, impact of women entering the labor force, industrial unionism

Immigration—Motives for immigration; immigrants' aspirations and expectations; the realities of working life for immigrants

Women's Rights—Critique of suffrage, women's liberation, birth control movement, motherhood and rearing of children, free love, sexuality, domestic inequality, discrimination in the workplace

World War I—Resistance to President Wilson's "preparedness" program, anti-conscription, conscientious objectors, economic analysis of the war effort, repression of dissent

Yellow Journalism—News coverage, political cartoons, identifying bias, popular fears of anarchism and women

Goldman was part of a blossoming culture of dissent. Her anarchism was one of many political philosophies of her time, including socialism, communism, utopianism, populism, and progressivism, that challenged and influenced the evolution of the dominant social and political culture. As an anarchist, Goldman maintained that social justice and individual freedom could not be legislated by the state. Instead, she argued that a complete transformation of social values and economic relations was needed.

In nationwide lecture tours, Goldman took her message to the people and in the process tested a democratic society's tolerance for dissent. Goldman believed that "the most violent element in society is ignorance." The government and most newspaper reporters responded fearfully to Goldman's iconoclastic ideas as well as to her confrontational style. She was shadowed by police and vigilantes determined to suppress her talks and was arrested frequently. In 1919, after spending a year and a half in prison for her open opposition to conscription and to U.S. entry into World War I, Goldman was deported.

Standard school texts often ignore Goldman and other challenging voices, or only briefly mention them. This absence of an historical record of controversy in the curriculum not only denies students access to a full range of ideas but also ultimately limits their ability to understand and analyze the past. Recent educational reforms encourage classroom use of primary sources as the best way to present opposing points of view. For example, the documents from the Emma

Goldman Papers on free speech are compelling because they expose the student to firsthand accounts of a long struggle to affirm the right to disagree. The immediacy of the issues of the period are experienced through newspaper accounts, political cartoons, speeches, pamphlets, and autobiographical narratives rather than through synthesized historical texts.

Using the Documents

The documents are organized into five topics:

Immigration
Freedom of Expression
Women's Rights
Anti-militarism
Art and Literature of Social Change

These topics can be taught in any sequence. The documents also may be used individually or in a combination of your choosing. The materials are appropriate for use by students individually, in small groups, or with the entire class.

The questions accompanying each document target a broad range of learning skills from recall to critical thinking. They provide the class with an opportunity to discuss both history and relevant current issues. The reading level varies among documents. The short biographical sketch is intended for easy reading; the fuller biographical essay is appropriate for more advanced students.

Documents were selected to suit the diverse learning styles and interests of 8th through 12th grade students. Each of the five topics includes suggested activities through which students may explore the broader significance of the documents and their context.

The Glossary defines terms that appear in the documents that may be unfamiliar to students. The Selected Resources section includes annotations on books, media, and literature.

Brief Introduction to Emma Goldman

Emma Goldman was born in the small city of Kovno in czarist Russia on June 27, 1869. As a child she and her family experienced blatant anti-Semitism and observed peasants beaten, government officials bribed, and young men dragged off to serve in the army. Hating the injustices she saw, she welcomed the idea of revolution that promised to change Russia. She hoped for a new world of equality and justice.

Goldman's family life was hard. Goldman felt that her father found fault with everything she did. He sent her out to work at an early age and wanted her to get married to someone of his choosing when she was only fifteen. To avoid such a future, Goldman and her older sister Helena fled Russia for America.

Full of optimism, she arrived in America in 1885 expecting to find the freedom she was denied back in Russia. Relatives in Rochester, New York, offered her a place to live and helped her find work in a clothing factory. Unhappily, she discovered that working conditions in America were not so different from those she had left behind.

Life changed dramatically for Goldman in 1886 when she read in the newspaper about an event at Haymarket Square in Chicago. It made her angry to learn that the police had attacked striking workers who were asking for an eight-hour workday. At a rally a bomb exploded and gunfire broke out, killing seven police officers. The city blamed anarchists for the bombing. A trial was held; eight men were found guilty, of whom four were executed in 1887. Goldman believed in the men's innocence. She began to read everything she could find on anarchism. Determined to make her adopted country live up to the ideals of freedom, harmony, and prosperity for all, Goldman left her sweatshop job in Rochester and went to New York City where she hoped to meet other people who shared her ideas. There she learned that anarchism had many definitions that spanned from philosophical to militant. She was attracted to those anarchists who lectured about the challenge and the promise of their political ideas. Yet the press often stereotyped the anarchist movement as "bomb-throwers" because some anarchists believed that political violence was a justifiable means for bringing about revolutionary change. Goldman found herself between these two poles.

Within New York's anarchist circle, Goldman befriended Alexander Berkman and was eventually associated with his attempt in 1892 to kill Henry Clay Frick, manager of a Carnegie Steel plant, after Frick had ordered an armed attack on striking workers. The newspapers sensationalized the event. Later, in 1901, when President William McKinley was assassinated by an anarchist, Goldman was suspected even though she was not involved. After this, Goldman briefly changed her name, led an underground life, and from then on was watched carefully by agents of the government. When it became safe for her to appear in public, she distinguished her conception of anarchism from the characterizations of it by the press. In 1906, she started the anarchist magazine *Mother Earth*. It gave writers, artists, and political thinkers with radical ideas a place to express themselves.

Among her many challenges to convention was Goldman's distrust of the institution of marriage. She thought that marriage restricted the freedom of both men and women and, at the same time, gave them a false sense of security. During her lifetime, she fell in love many times and had a ten-year love affair with her lecture tour manager, Dr. Ben Reitman. Even though she believed in the principle of free love, her letters to Ben show that she could not rid herself of her own feelings of jealousy when he followed his attraction to other women.

Goldman was a talented public speaker. She toured the country several times a year lecturing about politics, drama, birth control, economic freedom for women, education, anti-militarism, and other vital issues of her day. Goldman believed that anarchism would bring total social, economic, political, and spiritual emancipation without government control. Because of a common fear of anarchism, she faced constant threats from policemen and vigilantes determined to suppress her message. She was arrested countless times and spent over a year and a half in jail.

She spoke out against U.S. participation in World War I because she believed the war was being fought first and foremost to promote the economic interests of the very rich. In addition, she encouraged young men to resist compulsory military service. Arrested and convicted of conspiracy to obstruct the draft, she went to prison. During that time, her citizenship was invalidated by a government eager to rid the country of her influence. On December 21, 1919, Emma Goldman and 248 other foreign-born radicals were rushed aboard the ship S.S. *Buford* at dawn and deported to Soviet Russia.

Emma Goldman stayed in her native Russia for only twenty-three months. Despite the overthrow of the czar by a revolutionary government, Goldman was shocked by its continuing disregard for political freedom. She met with V. I. Lenin, the Soviet leader, and questioned him about the lack of free speech. Unhappy with his response that free speech at that point in Russian history was a luxury not a right, Goldman eventually left the country in disgust and disappointment. She was determined to alert the world to what she saw as the Bolsheviks' betrayal of the ideals of the revolution.

For the rest of her life Goldman felt like "a woman without a country," moving from place to place, and allowed to return to the United States only once in 1934 for a brief lecture tour. In 1936, she visited Spain and witnessed the optimism of the Spanish anarchists and their hope that a real revolution would occur in Spain during the Spanish Civil War. When the dictatorship of Francisco Franco triumphed, a defeated Goldman went to Canada to help raise funds for the refugees of the Spanish war and to be closer to the country in which she had felt most at home.

Emma Goldman died on May 14, 1940. The United States government permitted her body to be returned to America. She is buried in Chicago near the anarchists who were executed for the Haymarket incident.

Throughout her life Emma Goldman wrote many letters, articles, speeches, and a number of books. The most notable of her writings is her autobiography, *Living My Life*.

Timeline

1869	Emma Goldman born in Kovno, Lithuania.
1885	Goldman emigrates to the United States, settling in Rochester, N.Y.
1886	Haymarket bombing: At the height of the fight for the eight-hour work day, a bomb is thrown at police at a mass meeting in Haymarket Square, Chicago, to protest the police shooting the previous day of strikers at the McCormick Reaper Works. Though the culprit is never identified, eight anarchist leaders are tried for murder and found guilty.
1887	Goldman marries Jacob Kersner, gaining U.S. citizenship; unhappy in the marriage and attracted increasingly to anarchism, Goldman divorces Kersner within the year. Execution of four of the Haymarket anarchists.
1889	Goldman moves to New York City.
1890	Goldman's first lecture tour; speaks in Rochester, Buffalo, and Cleveland.
1892	Homestead, Pa., steel strike leads to a bloody confrontation between strikers and Pinkerton detectives; Goldman's comrade Alexander Berkman attempts to assassinate Henry Clay Frick, superintendent of the Carnegie Steel Company, and is sentenced to twenty-two years in prison; Goldman suspected of helping to plan the attempt on Frick's life.
1893	Goldman prosecuted for a speech at a demonstration of the unemployed in Union Square, New York City; found guilty of aiding and abetting an unlawful assembly; sentenced to one year in prison on Blackwell's Island, where she apprentices as a nurse to the inmates.
1894	Strike at the Pullman railroad car plant to protest layoffs and wage cuts spreads to many western railroads after the Pullman strikers appeal for support to American Railway Union leader Eugene Debs; strike is broken by court rulings against the union and by federal troops under orders from President Grover Cleveland.
1895-96	Goldman receives formal training in nursing in Vienna.
1898	Spanish-American War: the Philippines, Puerto Rico, and Guam ceded by Spain to the victorious United States.
1901	Assassination of President William McKinley by an anarchist. Goldman is unjustly implicated, arrested, held for questioning, and released. Goldman changes her name and, for a brief period, goes underground to avoid public harassment.
1903	Goldman helps found the Free Speech League in New York City in response to the first prosecution under a federal anti-anarchist law that barred anarchists from entering the country.

Timeline, continued

1905	Industrial Workers of the World (IWW) founded.
1906	*Mother Earth* magazine is founded by Emma Goldman and comrades; published until 1917.
1906	Goldman begins annual lecture tours to raise money for the magazine, speaking on a broad range of issues including modern European drama, women's equality and independence, sexuality and free love, child development and education, and religious fundamentalism. Alexander Berkman released from prison.
1908	Goldman denied the use of auditoriums in Chicago for meetings; meets Ben Reitman, who offers her his "Hobo Hall," and eventually becomes her lover and the manager of her lecture tours. IWW free speech fight in Missoula, Mont. (Free speech fights occurred often during this period when people like Goldman and organizations like the IWW tried to hold public meetings to express their views but were prevented from doing so by local authorities.)
1909	IWW free speech fight in Spokane, Washington.
1909-10	"Uprising of the Twenty Thousand," a general strike by women garment workers in New York City.
1910	Goldman's *Anarchism and Other Essays* published.
1911	Fire at the Triangle Shirtwaist Company in New York City kills 146 people, mostly young women, when exits that were kept locked to prevent union organizers from entering the premises prevented workers from escaping the fire, forcing many of them to jump to their deaths.
1912	Free speech fight in San Diego; Ben Reitman dragged from the city by vigilantes and brutalized. Lawrence, Mass., textile strike led by the IWW.
1913	IWW strike of Paterson, N.J., silk mills. Colorado coal strike to protest low pay, dangerous working conditions, and mine companies' domination of all aspects of workers' lives. The Armory show in New York City introduces European modern art to an American audience for the first time, creating a public scandal.
1914	Goldman's *Social Significance of the Modern Drama* published.

1914	Ludlow Massacre: Colorado National Guard troops and mine guards attack a tent colony inhabited by striking miners and their families; among the dead are two women and eleven children; in response, the miners mount an armed rebellion, which is crushed after ten days by federal troops. World War I begins in Europe.
1915-16	Goldman lectures frequently on birth control and is arrested several times; spends fifteen days in jail on one occasion for distributing birth control information.
1917	The United States declares war on Germany, entering World War I. Federal government imposes a draft. Goldman founds the No-Conscription League with Berkman, M. Eleanor Fitzgerald, and Leonard Abbott to oppose the draft. Goldman and Berkman tried and convicted for conspiracy to obstruct the draft, sentenced to two years imprisonment. Espionage Act passed.
1918	Sedition Act passed.
1918-19	Goldman serves time at state penitentiary in Jefferson City, Mo., Berkman in Atlanta federal penitentiary.
1919	Goldman and Berkman deported from the United States with 247 other alien radicals. (Goldman's husband had been denaturalized by the government in 1908 in order to deprive her of her citizenship. The 1918 Alien Act provided that an alien could be deported, if found to be an anarchist, at any time after entering the United States.)
1919-20	"Red Scare": In the United States, the intolerance and suspicion of foreigners and radicals increases in the postwar years as the Bolsheviks consolidate their victory in Russia, producing fear of worldwide revolution; climaxes in the 1920 Palmer raids, when thousands of foreign-born radicals are rounded up, and many deported.
1920	Nineteenth Amendment to the Constitution (giving women the right to vote) ratified. Sacco and Vanzetti, two Italian anarchists, arrested for the murder of a payroll guard in Massachusetts; the accused widely seen as victims of the anti-radical and anti-foreign sentiment of the period, an impression confirmed by the conduct of the trial.
1920-21	Goldman and Berkman in exile in Soviet Russia, where they confront the Bolsheviks' denial of free speech and expression and especially the suppression of anarchists.
1921	December: Goldman and Berkman leave Russia.

Timeline, continued

1922-24	Exile in Berlin, after a brief stay in Stockholm, Sweden.
1923	Goldman publishes *My Disillusionment in Russia.*
1924-26	Goldman lives in London, writing and lecturing on conditions in Soviet Russia and on modern drama.
1926-28	Goldman lives in Canada. Based in Toronto, she writes and lectures on Russia, modern drama, and social issues.
1927	Execution of anarchists Sacco and Vanzetti provokes international outcry.
1928-36	Goldman finds a base for her writing and a respite from her lecture tours in a cottage in Saint-Tropez, France, purchased for her by philanthropist Peggy Guggenheim.
1931	Goldman publishes her autobiography, *Living My Life*.
1932	Goldman lectures in Scandinavia and Germany on the menace of fascism and the rise of Nazism.
1933	Goldman expelled from Holland.
1934	Goldman granted a visa to enter the United States for a ninety-day lecture tour.
1936	Ill with cancer, Berkman commits suicide.
1936-38	Goldman visits Spain and enlists in the loyalist cause in the Spanish Civil War, later opening an office in London to raise support for the Spanish anarchists fighting on the loyalist side.
1939	Goldman moves to Canada after the defeat of the Spanish loyalists to raise funds for women and children refugees from the Civil War.
1940	Goldman dies in Toronto and is buried in Chicago near the Haymarket martyrs who first inspired her in 1887.

TOPIC ONE
Immigration

TOPIC ONE: Immigration

These documents refer to many issues about immigration that are as relevant today as they were in 1885 when the young Russian immigrant Emma Goldman arrived in America. They are:

- **Immigration policies**—what, when, and why people are admitted to or barred from the United States.

- **Adaptation**—how the immigrant adjusts to a new society and how the immigrant is accepted or rejected as a newcomer.

- **Diversity**—how much diversity a country can tolerate in maintaining a common culture.

- **Industrial labor**—the immigrant in the labor market, the issues of cheap labor, and the particular issues of a multicultural immigrant workforce.

Background to the documents: The first three documents in this section provide a dramatic point of introduction to Goldman—her deportation in 1919 to Soviet Russia. While the United States government over the years has deported only a small percentage of its millions of immigrants, nevertheless, deportation then and now is an element of American immigration policy.

Following World War I, high unemployment, labor unrest, and a growing intolerance for immigrants and their "foreign" ideas produced an atmosphere of heightened anti-radical feeling, commonly called the "Red Scare." The Russian Revolution of 1917 had increased fear in America that foreign-born radicals were planning to overthrow our government. U.S. Attorney General A. Mitchell Palmer and his special assistant J. Edgar Hoover gathered evidence against foreign-born radicals. Anarchists, who had been vocal in their opposition to World War I, were among the first groups to come under attack. In 1917, the office of Goldman's *Mother Earth* magazine was ransacked by government agents in search of incriminating evidence. On trial for opposing the draft, Goldman was imprisoned and her deportation was recommended. J. Edgar Hoover turned the deportation of Emma Goldman and her colleague Alexander Berkman into a personal crusade, calling them in an official letter "beyond doubt, two of the most dangerous anarchists in this country."

In spite of Goldman's insistence that she was a citizen and not an alien, the government invalidated her citizenship and then used the anti-anarchist immigration law as grounds for her deportation. This law prohibited entry into the United States of any person who did not believe in organized government.

Documents four and five reveal how Goldman, an immigrant worker in late nineteenth-century America, experienced the dehumanizing effects of sweatshop labor in the textile industry.

Document One
Political cartoon

"Uncle Sam bids good riddance to the deportees"
(from J. Edgar Hoover's memorabilia and scrapbook in the National Archives)

Context: World War I and the Russian Revolution created a climate of fear in the United States directed against those identified as foreign-born radicals. One government tactic to rid the country of these people included deportation. On December 21, 1919, 249 radicals were deported from the United States to the Soviet Union aboard the S.S. *Buford*—often referred to as the "Red Ark." Emma Goldman and her comrade Alexander Berkman were the most notorious among the deportees. Present at the dock was the young J. Edgar Hoover, head of the Justice Department's General Intelligence Division. Hoover, who had turned the deportation of Goldman and Berkman into a personal crusade, labeled them "two of the most dangerous anarchists in this country."

Questions on the Document:
Read the cartoon: Who is on the ship? Where are they going?
How does the cartoon portray the deportees?
Suggest some adjectives that describe the emotions elicited in the cartoon.
Who is Uncle Sam? What does Uncle Sam mean? What attitude does the phrase "good riddance" express?

General Questions:
What does it mean to be deported?
Would this cartoon be popular today?
Suggest another time in American history when the attitudes expressed in this cartoon would be relevant.
Does the U.S. government deport people today? Give some examples of recent instances of deportation. For what reasons were these people sent back to the country they came from? Were these reasons political? economic? racial?
How has immigration policy changed since 1919?

Uncle Sam Bids Good Riddance to the Deportees

Document Two

a. Emma Goldman's written recollections of her arrival in and deportation from the United States from her autobiography, *Living My Life*

b. Photograph of Goldman at age seventeen

c. Goldman's official deportation portrait

Context: In her autobiography, *Living My Life*, Emma Goldman describes her feelings as a seventeen-year-old arriving in a new country and her feelings as a fifty-year-old woman upon her deportation from the United States.

Questions on the Document:
What thoughts about the world did Goldman have on the day of her departure?
What words describe the sounds and atmosphere of the deportation? What mood do they create?
How do you think she was feeling? Why?
What thoughts about the United States did she have on the day she arrived?
How was she feeling then? Why?
Compare her thoughts as her boat passes the Statue of Liberty in 1886 and in 1919.
Speculate on her life in America in the years between these two events.

General Questions:
Today, where and how do people entering the United States arrive?
Do people today have the same reasons for immigrating to America as they did in the past?
Identify some reasons.
For what reasons would you emigrate? To what country would you go?

Emma Goldman recounts the day of her arrival in the United States in 1885:

My first contact with the sea was terrifying and fascinating. The freedom from home, the beauty and wonder of the endless expanse in its varying moods, and the exciting anticipation of what the new land would offer stimulated my imagination and sent my blood tingling.... Helena and I stood pressed to each other, enraptured by the sight of the harbour and the Statue of Liberty suddenly emerging from the mist. Ah, there she was, the symbol of hope, of freedom, of opportunity! She held her torch high to light the way to the free country, the asylum for the oppressed of all lands. We, too, Helena and I, would find a place in the generous heart of America. Our spirits were high, our eyes filled with tears.

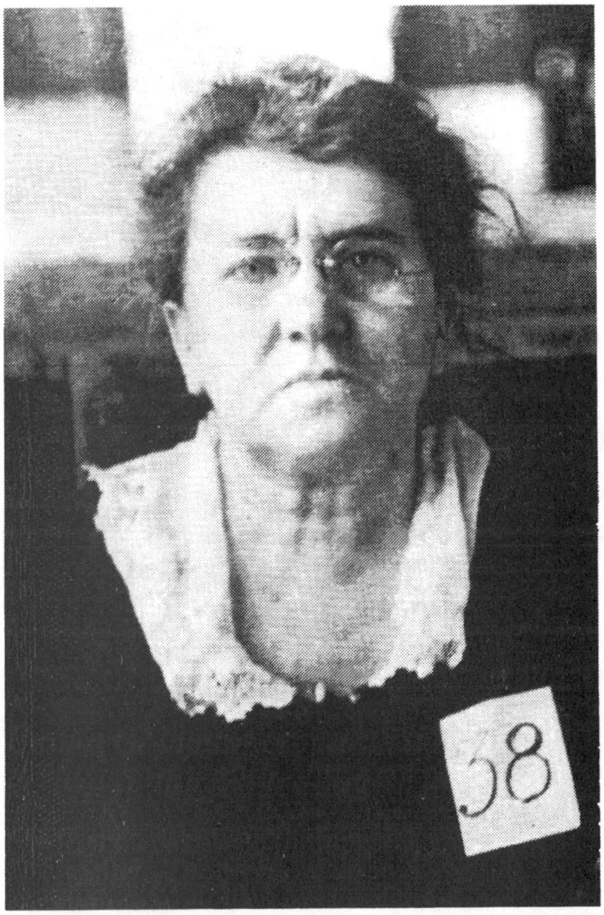

...and the day of her deportation in 1919:

It was almost midnight when suddenly I caught the sound of approaching footsteps. "Look out someone's coming!" Ethel whispered. I snatched up my papers and letters and hid them under my pillow. Then we threw ourselves on our beds, covered up, and pretended to be asleep.

The steps halted at our room. There came the rattling of keys; the door was unlocked and noisily thrown open. Two guards and a matron entered. "Get up now," they commanded, "get your things ready!"...

Deep snow lay on the ground; the air was cut by a biting wind. A row of armed civilians and soldiers stood along the road to the bank. Dimly the outlines of a barge were visible through the morning mist. One by one the deportees marched, flanked on each side by the uniformed men, curses and threats accompanying the thud of their feet on the frozen ground. When the last man had crossed the gangplank, the girls and I were ordered to follow, officers in front and in back of us....

I looked at my watch. It was 4:20 A.M. on the day of our Lord, December 21, 1919. On the deck above us I could hear the men tramping up and down in the wintry blast. I felt dizzy, visioning a transport of politicals doomed to Siberia, the *étape* of former Russian days. Russia of the past rose before me and I saw the revolutionary martyrs being driven into exile. But no, it was New York, it was America, the land of liberty! Through the port-hole I could see the great city receding into the distance, its sky-line of buildings traceable by their rearing heads. It was my beloved city, the metropolis of the New World. It was America, indeed, America repeating the terrible scenes of tsarist Russia! I glanced up—the Statue of Liberty!

Excerpted from *Living My Life* (p. 11, pp. 716-717).
Photo credits: International Institute of Social History, Amsterdam

Document Three

New York Tribune article, "Anarchists Likely To Be Put on Ship Bound for Russia" December 5, 1919

Context: The Red Scare was a time when the federal government cracked down on the activities of radicals. Based on the recommendation of federal commissions and investigative committees, Congress tried to restrict the entry of immigrants who held radical ideas. To rid itself of radicals already living in the United States, the government also deported those who lived in the United States but were not citizens.

Questions on the Document:

In your own words, summarize the following topics that appear in the article: 1) ...a surprise is in store for the anarchists..., 2) Destination in Question, 3) Anarchistic Teachings Found in Library, 4) Mislig Defies Committee.
What basis for government fears about radical expression is reported in this article?
What political situation in Soviet Russia caused Goldman and Berkman to be worried?
What were Representative Siegel's concerns? What remedy do you think he will recommend?
Why do you think Michael Mislig declined to give the Lusk Committee the names of members of the Russian Socialist Federation?
What attitudes about Russian immigrants does this article reveal?

General Questions:

What was the U.S. relationship to the Bolshevik government in 1919?
Were immigrants a particular target during the "Red Scare"?
How do you characterize the political climate in the United States in 1919 based on this one newspaper report?
What other repressive acts did the government take during the period known as the "Red Scare"?

Anarchists Likely to Be Put on Ship Bound for Russia as They Start for Ellis Island To-day

Seek Habeas Corpus Writ

Books Teaching Anarchy Found in Harlem Public Library, Says Siegel

The little tug which plies between the Battery and Ellis Island will leave its wharf at the foot of Broadway promptly at 11 o'clock this morning, carrying Emma Goldman and Alexander Berkman, anarchists, on the first lap of their long journey to Russia. According to Federal officials, it will be the last time Miss Goldman and Berkman will set foot on the mainland of the United States, where for years they have preached anarchist propaganda.

Intimations that a surprise is in store for the anarchists when they arrive at the island were made yesterday by Byron H. Uhl, Acting Commissioner of Immigration.

"I understand the government has something up its sleeve, but I don't know just what it is," he said. Other officials declared they believed the order deporting Miss Goldman and Berkman calls for their immediate transfer to a ship bound for Russia.

Destination in Question

Differences of opinion have arisen between Mr. Uhl and Harry Weinberger, counsel for the anarchists, relative to what part of Russia the two aliens are to be sent. Mr. Weinberger disclosed a telegram from Anthony Caminetti, Commissioner of Immigration, stating that Miss Goldman and Berkman would be sent to Soviet Union.

"I have been promised by more than one government official that they will be delivered to Bolshevik officials," said Mr. Weinberger. "It would mean their murder to deliver them into the hands of anti-Bolshevik forces."

Mr. Uhl contended the anarchists cannot be sent to Soviet Russia because this government has not recognized the Soviet government. "The law provides for deportation to the countries from whence the aliens came," he said. "They can be deported regardless of changes of government."

Mr. Weinberger said he still had hopes of obtaining writs of habeas corpus, which would act as a stay against the deportation. He said he would contend that Miss Goldman is an American citizen through marriage. Berkman's defense is he has ceased to be an anarchist.

Anarchistic Teachings Found in Library

Representative Isaac Siegel, after a trip to Ellis Island yesterday, declared he had discovered how anarchists are made. Mr. Siegel is a member of the House Congressional Committee appointed to investigate conditions at the Island.

"Books in our public libraries help to make anarchists," he said. "I found a boy on the Island—Thomas Buhokanob, seventeen years old, a native of Russia, who came here seven years ago. He was educated in Public School 38. He read anarchist books out of the Harlem Public Library. Then he helped circulate Emma Goldman's 'Mother Earth.' After that he went to Greenpoint, where he organized Russians who could not speak English and taught them what he had learned about anarchy.

"He told me he did not believe in the Constitution, in any form of government or in God."

Mr. Siegel said the committee would meet in Washington on Monday, when it will question Secretary of Labor Wilson, Louis F. Post, Assistant Secretary of the Department of Labor, and other officials.

Mislig Defies Committee

The Lusk Legislative Committee devoted its session yesterday to obtaining the political views of Dr. Michael Mislig, formerly treasurer of the Russian Socialist Federation. He declined to tell the committee the names of the federation's executive committee, although Assemblyman Louis Martin warned him he would be in contempt.

Ernest Albert Kurth, who was indicted on a charge of assault with intent to kill for having sent a bomb concealed in a tin candy box to Mrs. Rodman Wanamaker, pleaded guilty yesterday before Judge William H. Wadhams in General Sessions. He will be sentenced December 11.

New York Tribune, *Dec. 5, 1919*

Document Four

On Becoming an Anarchist

a. Excerpt from "Was My Life Worth Living?" (1934)

b. Goldman Family Photograph, St. Petersburg, 1882

c. Illustration of Haymarket Martyrs by Walter Crane, 1894

Context: On June 27, 1869, Goldman's life began in a small imperial Russian city, now in the Republic of Lithuania. Her family, living in Jewish ghettos and moving often in search of employment, suffered the anti-Semitism of the times. At age twelve Goldman was exposed to the growing revolution in Russia with its promise to end the tremendous inequities of the old order under the Czar.

Goldman's formal schooling ended when her father put her to work full time in a corset factory. He wanted her to marry a man of his choosing, which was the custom of the time. Fifteen-year-old Goldman rejected his demands, protesting that above all, she wanted an opportunity to study. Angrily, her father told her, "Girls do not have to learn much, only how to prepare minced fish, cut noodles fine, and give the man plenty of children!"

Determined to escape her father's authority, she and her half-sister Helena set sail for America in 1885. In her article "Was My Life Worth Living?" written in 1934 after her brief tour of the United States, she reflects upon her life in Russia and her first years as an immigrant in the United States.

Questions on the document:
What did Goldman rebel against?
Do you think that Goldman's decision to immigrate was common for single women in her day? Would you have made the same choice?
What picture of democracy did immigrants from Europe have?
What disillusioned Goldman about America?

General Questions:
What dreams might immigrants coming to America have today? What disillusionment might they experience?
Do you see any differences in social and economic conditions for immigrants today compared to Goldman's day?
Do you think that male and female immigrants face different problems in adjusting to American society? Explain.

Excerpt from "Was My Life Worth Living?"

by Emma Goldman.

Since my earliest recollection of my youth in Russia I have rebelled against orthodoxy in every form. I could never bear to witness harshness whether on the part of our parents to us or in their dealings with the servants. I was outraged over the official brutality practiced on the peasants in our neighborhood. I wept bitter tears when the young men were conscripted into the army and torn from homes and hearths. I resented the treatment of our servants, who did the hardest work and yet had to put up with wretched sleeping quarters and the leavings of our table. I was indignant when I discovered that love between young people of Jewish and Gentile origin was considered the crime of crimes, and the birth of an illegitimate child the most depraved immorality.

On coming to America I had the same hopes as have most European immigrants and the same disillusionment, though the latter affected me more keenly and more deeply. The immigrant without money and without connections is not permitted to cherish the comforting illusion that America is a benevolent uncle who assumes a tender and impartial guardianship of nephews and nieces. I soon learned that in a republic there are myriad ways by which the strong, the cunning, the rich can seize power and hold it. I saw the many work for small wages which kept them always on the borderline of want for the few who made huge profits. I saw the courts, the halls of legislation, the press, and the schools—in fact every avenue of education and protection—effectively used as an instrument for the safeguarding of a minority, while the masses were denied every right. I found that the politicians knew how to befog every issue, how to control public opinion and manipulate votes to their own advantage and to that of their financial and industrial allies. This was the picture of democracy I soon discovered on my arrival in the United States. Fundamentally there have been few changes since that time.

This situation, which was a matter of daily experience, was brought home to me with a force that tore away shams and made reality stand out vividly and clearly by an event which occurred shortly after my coming to America. It was the so-called Haymarket riot, which

The Goldman family in St. Petersburg, 1882: Emma, Helena, Morris (in Helena's lap), Taube, Herman, and Abraham. (New York Public Library)

resulted in the trial and conviction of eight men, among them five Anarchists. Their crime was an all-embracing love for their fellow-men and their determination to emancipate the oppressed and disinherited masses. In no way had the State of Illinois succeeded in proving their connection with the bomb that had been thrown at an open-air meeting in Haymarket Square in Chicago. It was their Anarchism which resulted in their conviction and execution on the 11th of November, 1887. This judicial crime left an indelible mark on my mind and heart and sent me forth to acquaint myself with the ideal for which these men had died so heroically. I dedicated myself to their cause.

Published in Harper's Monthly Magazine, *December 1934, pp. 52-58.*

"The Anarchists of Chicago"
Memorial drawing by Walter Crane, 1894 (Haymarket Scrapbook)

Document Five

a. Excerpt from *Living My Life* on Goldman's factory-working experience

b. Illustration of clothing-work factory, *New York Weekly* (1871)

Context: Many women immigrants like Goldman found poorly paid work in unsafe and unhealthy sweatshops and textile factories in northeastern cities. Goldman's first experience working in Rochester, New York, led her to believe that conditions in America were little better than in Russia.

Questions on the document:
Describe the working conditions to which Goldman objected.
If you had been an immigrant at the time, would you have spoken out against such conditions? What might the consequences of such action have been?
What was Mr. Garson's response to Goldman's request for a raise?
How does Goldman's description of Garson's office and her confrontation with him dramatize the disparity between workers and owners in industrial America?
What specific aspects of factory labor restricted Goldman's sense of freedom?
What does this account reveal about Goldman's personality? What type of person do you think she was?

General Questions:
What type of jobs are available today for immigrants in your area? Why?
What tensions in society have arisen over the issue of hiring immigrants instead of American citizens?
What are examples of the positive influences of immigrants on the economy, politics, and culture of American society?

Conditions in a "model" factory

Now I was in America, in the Flower City of the State of New York, in a model factory, as I was told. Certainly, Garson's clothing-works were a vast improvement on the glove factory on the Vassilevsky Ostrov. The rooms were large, bright, and airy. One had elbow space. There were none of those ill-smelling odours that used to nauseate me in our cousin's shop. Yet the work here was harder, and the day, with only half an hour for lunch, seemed endless. The iron discipline forbade free movement (one could not even go to the toilet without permission), and the constant surveillance of the foreman weighed like stone on my heart. The end of each day found me sapped, with just enough energy to drag myself to my sister's home and crawl into bed. This continued with deadly monotony week after week.

The amazing thing to me was that no one else in the factory seemed to be so affected as I, no one but my neighbour, frail little Tanya. She was delicate and pale, frequently complained of headaches, and often broke into tears when the task of handling heavy ulsters proved too much for her. One morning, as I looked up from my work, I discovered her all huddled in a heap. She had fallen in a faint. I called to the foreman to help me carry her to the dressing-room, but the deafening noise of the machines drowned my voice. Several girls near by heard me and began to shout. They ceased working and rushed over to Tanya. The sudden stopping of the machines attracted the foreman's attention and he came over to us. Without even asking the reason for the commotion, he shouted, "Back to your machines! What do you mean stopping work now? Do you want to be fired? Get back at once!" When he spied the crumpled body of Tanya, he yelled: "What the hell is the matter with her?" "She has fainted," I replied, trying hard to control my voice. "Fainted, nothing," he sneered, "she's only shamming."

"You are a liar and a brute!" I cried, no longer able to keep back my indignation.

I bent over Tanya, loosened her waist, and squeezed the juice of an orange I had in my lunch basket into her half-opened mouth. Her face was white, a cold sweat on her forehead. She looked so ill that even the foreman realized she had not been shamming. He excused her for the day. "I will go with Tanya," I said; "you can deduct from my pay for the time." "You can go to hell, you wildcat!" he flung after me.

We went to a coffee place. I myself felt empty and faint, but all we had between us was seventy-five cents. We decided to spend forty on food, and use the rest for a street-car ride to the park. There, in the fresh air, amid the flowers and trees, we forgot our dreaded tasks. The day that had begun in trouble ended restfully and in peace.

The next morning the enervating routine started all over again, continuing for weeks and months, broken only by the new arrival in our family, a baby girl. The child became the one interest in my dull existence. Often, when the atmosphere in Garson's factory threatened to overcome me, the thought of the lovely mite at home revived my spirit The evenings were no longer dreary and meaningless. But, while little Stella brought joy into our household, she added to the material anxiety of my sister and my brother-in-law.

Excerpt from *Living My Life* (volume 1, pp. 16-17)

I apply for a rise in salary

Lena never by word or deed made me feel that the dollar and fifty cents I was giving her for my board (the car fare amounted to sixty cents a week, the remaining forty cents being my pin-money) did not cover my keep. But I had overheard my brother-in-law grumbling over the growing expenses of the house. I felt he was right. I did not want my sister worried, she was nursing her child. I decided to apply for a rise. I knew it was no use talking to the foreman and therefore I asked to see Mr. Garson.

I was ushered into a luxurious office. American Beauties were on the table. Often I had admired them in the flower shops, and once, unable to withstand the temptation, I had gone in to ask the price. They were one dollar and a half apiece—more than half of my week's earnings. The lovely vase in Mr. Garson's office held a great many of them.

I was not asked to sit down. For a moment I forgot my mission. The beautiful room, the roses, the aroma of the bluish smoke from Mr. Garson's cigar, fascinated me. I was recalled to reality by my employer's question: "Well, what can I do for you?"

I had come to ask for a rise, I told him. The two dollars and a half I was getting did not pay my board, let along anything else, such as an occasional book or a theatre ticket for twenty-five cents. Mr. Garson replied that for a factory girl I had rather extravagant tastes, that all his "hands" were well satisfied, that they seemed to be getting along all right—that I, too, would have to manage or find work elsewhere. "If I raise your wages, I'll have to raise the others' as well and I can't afford that," he said. I decided to leave Garson's employ.

STREET AND SMITH'S

NEW YORK WEEKLY

BERTHA, THE SEWING-MACHINE GIRL:

OR

DEATH AT THE WHEEL.

By FRANCIS S. SMITH.

New York Weekly, May 23, 1871

Topic One: Immigration
Suggested Activities

Create a radio drama complete with sound effects using the accounts from Document Two.

Portray Goldman's arrival, her work in a textile factory, and her deportation in a dramatic presentation.

Draw a political cartoon about the "Red Scare."

Find information or photographs pertaining to Ellis Island and the Statue of Liberty. Design an exhibit with captions that explain how these symbols have been meaningful to immigrants.

Look up the terms *alien, deportee*, and *habeas corpus*. Explain how they are used in the documents.

Hold a debate on the issue of immigration quotas versus "open" immigration.

Locate some Lewis Hine photographs. Find some contemporary photographs of immigrant workers to compare and contrast with Hine's images. Use all of the images to create a presentation on the theme of immigrant working conditions.

Research the latest immigration statistics to determine:

a) How many people immigrate to the United States annually?
b) From which countries do they emigrate?
c) What motivates immigrants to come to the United States?

Using graphs and charts, compare your findings about recent immigration with immigration patterns in Goldman's time (between 1890 and 1920). What is similar? What is different?

Design a questionnaire to evaluate the experience of recent immigrants to your school or community. Conduct a survey and report on your findings.

TOPIC TWO

Freedom of Expression

TOPIC TWO: Freedom of Expression

This section explores the theme of freedom of expression. It examines such topics as:

- Anarchism—the anarchist's definition of individual expression and government's reaction.
- Free Speech—differing perceptions and limits to free speech.
- The First Amendment—struggles to defend it and efforts to restrict its guarantees.
- Vigilantism—force and violence as a tactic of societal control.
- Media—journalistic bias in writing and in visual images.

Background to the documents: The inequities that resulted from unrestricted industrial capitalism aroused criticism from many social observers. Plans for reform included calls for radical change. Emma Goldman called for revolutionary change rather than reform of the existing system. As an anarchist she envisioned a social order based on individual liberty and consensus unrestricted by law. She asserted in her autobiography, *Living My Life,* "I want freedom, the right to self-expression, everybody's right to beautiful, radiant things." The first documents in this section help explain Emma Goldman's attraction to and definition of anarchism and her experiences as an advocate of free speech. In Document Six a romantic portrayal of the anarchist vision of the New World is illustrated in a *Mother Earth* cover. Documents Seven through Nine provide news accounts and political cartoons that convey the range of the public's perception and fears about Goldman, anarchists, and anarchism in general.

Believing deeply in anarchism's promise to transform society, Goldman became one of its most well-known spokespersons. A charismatic speaker, she called upon Americans to exercise fully their rights to self-expression. Her message challenged conventional morality and threatened political stability. She faced constant threats from police and vigilantes determined to suppress her talks. Undeterred by her many arrests and imprisonments, Goldman continued to assert her constitutional right to free speech.

Following the assassination of President McKinley in 1901 by an anarchist, tolerance for free speech declined further. Liberal and radical Americans reacted angrily by becoming more vocal in their opposition to the abridgement of First Amendment rights. The government's attempts to suppress Goldman's unconventional views often backfired, and led many who disagreed with her ideas to support her right to express them freely. Document Ten highlights Emma Goldman's warning to the nation that restriction of the free expression of radical ideas would have serious consequences for the future of democracy in America. Document Eleven reveals organizational efforts to support the exercise of free speech. Document Twelve describes the free speech fight in San Diego, California, in 1912. In Document Thirteen Goldman challenges the Bolshevik repression of anarchists in Soviet Russia in a meeting with Lenin.

Document Six
Goldman's Definition of Anarchism

a. *Mother Earth* cover, *1906*

b. Excerpts from *Anarchism and Other Essays* by Emma Goldman

Context: This illustration appeared on the cover of the first issue of Goldman's anarchist magazine, *Mother Earth*. The magazine published writings on anarchism, news of national and international anarchist and labor activities, and poetry and drama criticism.

Questions on the Document:
Describe, in your own words, Goldman's definitions of anarchism.
Based on what you have learned about Goldman's definition of anarchism, what symbols in the picture are intended to illustrate the concepts of anarchism?

General Questions:
Which medium do you think conveys the power and meaning of a complex political vision more effectively—the written word or visual imagery? Explain.
Does your textbook include the term *anarchist* or *anarchism*? How is it defined?
Compare and contrast the definition of *anarchism* with your textbook's definition of the terms *communism* and *socialism*, if they are included.
Name some examples of the use of any of these terms in today's world—in slogans, graffiti, music lyrics, groups, etc. Does the meaning of the words change in different contexts?

Emma Goldman's definition of anarchism
(excerpts from *Anarchism and Other Essays*)

Mother Earth cover, May 1906

"I shall begin with a definition:
Anarchism:
The philosophy of a new social order
based on liberty unrestricted by
man-made law;
the theory that all forms of government
rest on violence,
and are therefore wrong and harmful,
as well as unnecessary."

"Anarchism, then, really stands for the
liberation of the human mind
from the dominion of religion;
the liberation of the human body
from the dominion of property:
liberation from the shackles
and restraint of government.
Anarchism stands for a social order
based on the free grouping of individuals for
the purpose of producing real social wealth;
an order that will guarantee to every human
being free access
to the earth and full enjoyment
of the necessities of life,
according to individual desires,
tastes, and inclinations."

"Anarchism
is the great, surging, living truth
that is reconstructing the world,
and that will usher in the Dawn."

Document Seven

Chicago Daily Tribune article, "Emma Goldman, High Priestess of Anarchy, Whose Speeches Inspired Czolgosz to His Crime," with illustration, September 8, 1901

Context: On September 6, 1901, anarchist Leon Czolgosz attempted to assassinate President William McKinley. Although Emma Goldman did not know Czolgosz and opposed assassination as a political tactic, she was implicated and arrested as a co-conspirator. Because Czolgosz had attended one of Goldman's speeches, the press blamed Goldman for the attempt on the President's life. The assassination incident increased the people's belief that anarchism was a philosophy of violence. This demonic portrayal of Goldman illustrates the prevailing perception of women who take on a public political role as either devils or angels.

Questions on the Document:
What does the illustration and headline say about the press response to the assassination attempt?
What does Goldman say about violence?
Do you think this speech could incite violence? Do you believe that a person who makes such a speech is responsible for violence that might result?
Do you think that a speech can incite violence?
Were the anarchists the only people who believed in direct action? What other reform groups engaged in direct action?

General Questions:
Find other historical examples of American political leaders who have been assassinated or who have had attempts made on their lives.
Do such incidents affect the country's general perception of democracy and freedoms granted in the Bill of Rights?—freedom of assembly, the right to bear arms, freedom of speech.
Is assassination of a political figure ever justifiable? Explain your response.
What other avenues are open for expressing dissent and effecting change? In your opinion, are they adequate? What are your ideas about government leadership and accountability?

EMMA GOLDMAN, HIGH PRIESTESS OF ANARCHY, WHOSE SPEECHES INSPIRED CZOLGOSZ TO HIS CRIME.

SPEECH THAT PROMPTED MURDEROUS ASSAULT ON THE PRESIDENT.

See next page for an account of Goldman's speech from *Chicago Daily Tribune*, Sept. 8, 1901.

SPEECH THAT PROMPTED MURDEROUS ASSAULT ON THE PRESIDENT.

Cleveland. O. Sept. 7 — [Special] — An address delivered in this city on May 6 by Emma Goldman, the Anarchist, is believed largely responsible for the attempt on the life of President McKinley.

Miss Goldman spoke here twice on that date, and a copy of her address was found in the pocket of Leon Czolgosz when searched by the Buffalo police. In the audience on that occasion was the man who tried to kill the President, and his associates now recall that he was one of the most enthusiastic in his applause of the utterances of Miss Goldman.

The hall in which the lecture was delivered is at 170 Superior street, the same hall in which the Anarchists now meet in this city.

In the course of her address of May 6, Miss Goldman first outlined the principles of anarchy and detailed the methods whereby she hoped to accomplish the ends of anarchy. Her talk was full of forceful passages, and some cases more notable for their strength than for their elegance.

"Men under the present state of society," she said, "are mere products of circumstances. Under the galling yoke of government, ecclesiasticism, and a bond of custom and prejudice, it is impossible for the individual to work out his own career as he could wish. Anarchism aims at a new and complete freedom. It strives to bring about the freedom which is not only the freedom from within but a freedom from without, which will prevent any man from having a desire to interfere in any way with the liberty of his neighbor.

"Vanderbilt says, 'I am a free man within myself, but the others be damned.' This is not the freedom we are striving for. We merely desire complete individual liberty, and this can never be obtained as long as there is an existing government.

"We do not favor the socialistic idea of converting men and women into mere producing machines under the eye of a paternal govenment. We go to the opposite extreme and demand the fullest and most complete liberty for each and every person to work out his own salvation upon any line that he pleases. The degrading notions of men and women as machines is far from our ideals of life.

"Anarchism has nothing to do with future governments or economic arrangements. We do not favor any particular settlement in this line, but merely ask to do away with the present evils. The future will provide these arrangements after our work has been done. Anarchism deals merely with social relations, and not with economic arrangement."

The speaker then deprecated the idea that all Anarchists were in favor of violence or bomb throwing. She declared that nothing was further from the principles they support. She went on, however, into a detailed explanation of the different crimes committed by Anarchists lately, declaring that the motive was good in each case, and that these acts were merely a matter of temperament.

Some men were so constituted, she said, that they were unable to stand idly by and see the wrong that was being endured by their fellow-mortals. She herself did not believe in these methods, but she did not think they should be condemned in view of the high and noble motives which prompted their perpetration. She continued: "Some believe we should first obtain by force and let the intelligence and education come afterwards."

Miss Goldman did not hesitate to put forward a number of sentiments far more radical and sensational than any ever publicly advanced here. During Miss Goldman's lecture a strong detail of police was in the hall to keep her from uttering sentiments which were regarded as too radical. This accounts for the fact that the speaker did not give free rein to her thoughts on this occasion. By reason of anarchistic uprisings elsewhere it was thought best by the city officials to curb the utterances of the woman.

Chicago Daily Tribune, *Sept. 8, 1901*

Document Eight

Political cartoons

Context: Many Americans drew their images of radicals from cartoons like these published in newspapers. Sometimes increasing sales with sensationalized news seemed more important to newspapers of the period than the truth and accuracy of their journalism. The press frequently seized the opportunity to sensationalize not only Goldman's anarchist perspective, but also the particular spectacle of a woman assuming a prominent role in the public arena.

Questions on the Document:
Read each cartoon and explain its message.
What image of the anarchist emerges? What words are used to describe anarchists?
How might these images have influenced public opinion?
What does the cartoon suggest Uncle Sam will need to do?
Who do you think might have agreed with the cartoon? Who would have disagreed? Why?

"Lock on mouth cartoon":
What is happening in the cartoon? What is the policeman preventing Goldman from doing?

General Questions:
Can a political cartoon be unbiased? Explain.
Name some political cartoonists who are popular today. Why do you think their cartoons are popular?
Besides cartoons, what other forms of political commentary rely on humor to make their point?
Do you think that there are topics that should not be the subject of humor or satire? Why or why not?

Kansas State Historical Collection

Kansas State Historical Collection

NOW HE WILL HAVE TO ACT

He stood by and placidly watched his country become infected with the germs of the earth.

From the Yiddish Press, c. 1901

Document Nine

San Francisco Call Editorial, "The Spirit of Anarchy," September 29, 1901

Context: This editorial was reprinted in 1901 following Goldman's implication in the assassination of President William McKinley. The editorial first appeared in 1898 in response to one of Emma Goldman's visits to San Francisco where she publicly denounced both the Spanish-American War and President William McKinley.

Questions on the Document:
What is the editor's attitude toward anarchists?
How does the editor define anarchism?
What values does the editor defend?
How would an anarchist respond to the editor's attitude toward workers?
Contrast the editor's definition of civilization with the anarchist definition as suggested by the *Mother Earth* cover.
How was the anarchist position on the role of government different from other social change movements of the period?

General Questions:
What is an editorial? How does it differ from a news article?
Do newspapers have political biases? How can you determine a bias?
Is T.V. programming free from bias? Depending on your opinion, give examples.
What is needed to create a balanced presentation on a topic?

THE SAN FRANCISCO CALL, SUNDAY, SEPTEMBER 29, 1901

THE SAN FRANCISCO CALL

JOHN D. SPRECKELS, Proprietor. Address Communications to W. S. LEAKE, Manager

SUNDAY .... SEPTEMBER 29, 1901

Publication Office .... Market and Third, S. F.

THE SPIRIT OF ANARCHY.

The record of several anarchists who by bomb-throwing and other forms of assassination have brought themselves into position in which their lives could be laid bare furnishes an interesting study.

They have usually been found to have lived in violation of the moral law which was in force among men before national codes were formed, and is understood to restrain men even when they are beyond the reach of codes and statutes. Their domestic relations are frequently illicit and their ideas of rights of property are not derived from the ten commandments.

As organized society and the laws of states are based upon the rights of person and property and defend the moral foundation of the domestic relations, anarchy hits its hand against society and against government.

When confronted with such records as are revealed by the arrest of anarchists who have been guilty of assassination it is their practice to reply that the moral offenses committed by them are also practiced by others who profess to support organized society and to support government.

That is obviously true. But such violators of the moral code are secret sinners, who realize their offense and conceal it and shrink from making its practice the social rule by the destruction of government and its institutions.

The spirit of anarchy is one that resists moral restraint, that chafes under the discipline of institutions, and strikes impartiality at church and state, because each is in its way the agent of morality and discipline.

It would seem, then, that anarchy is the cult of the abnormal man, of the class of atavists who reject everything that has come into the world with civilization.

Those who publicly propagate it are the apostles of crime, the evangelists of assassination.

Their cry to the laboring man is that he is a slave, and no means are omitted to embitter him and make him an agent in the destruction of civilization and government.

It needs no profound knowledge or exalted intelligence to discern the motives or deny the premises of anarchy. Modern civilization, which it attacks, has lifted the face of labor from the ground and turned it toward the stars. It has taken labor in the mass out of serfdom into independence, out of a hut into a house. It has dotted the nations with schools wherein the sons and daughters of laboring men have been freely offered the opportunity for a better education than was within the reach of princes a thousand years ago.

Government and civilization have put the personal and property rights of labor on exactly the same footing and under the same judicial protection as the rights of the rich, born in the purple.

The improved economic conditions, due to modern civilization, have put over labor a shelter, into its life comforts, and on its table food that were the exclusive possession of royalty and nobility five hundred years ago.

So government and social institutions can point to what they have done for the enfranchisement of man since the dark ages. To what can anarchy point as its achievements for humanity? To the innocent torn to shreds by dynamite; to the President of a republic murdered in his carriage; to the Czar who decreed freedom and ownership of land to 25,000,000 serfs, assassinated in the streets of St. Petersburg; to a score of faithful policemen murdered in Haymarket square while doing their duty as protectors of person and property. What has all this crime and violence done for labor? Has it given wages, shelter, food and schooling? Has it advanced man a step in the path of further progress which civilization has opened for him?

Let it blazon its achievements and inform labor of the mighty things it has wrought for those who toil that the world may strike a balance between murder and civilization as a means for the uplifting of the race.

San Francisco Call, *April 28, 1898, reprinted Sept. 29, 1901*

Document Ten

Letter from Emma Goldman to the Editor of *Lucifer the Lightbearer* (1902)

Context: Goldman's letter to the editor was published on December 11, 1902, in the anarchist periodical *Lucifer the Lightbearer*. It alerts readers to the continued police harassment surrounding her lectures and draws ominous conclusions about the future of First Amendment rights in America.

Questions on the Document:
What happened in Chicago that prompted Goldman to write this letter?
What kind of picture of life in Czarist Russia in 1902 does Goldman portray in her account?
What are the connections she draws between her treatment by the authorities in the United States with the suppression of free speech in Czarist Russia?
What did Goldman predict as the consequences of continued suppression of free speech?
What actions did she suggest as a remedy to the problems surrounding the issue of free speech in America? Why?

General Questions:
Which constitutional amendment guarantees the right of free speech? What does it say?
Are there limits to free speech? Under what circumstances and why?
In your opinion, is graffiti a form of free speech?
What is your opinion about the constitutional right of musical groups, like 2 Live Crew, to express any opinions they want in their lyrics?
What reception would Emma Goldman's ideas receive in your city council meetings today?

Price 8 Cents

LUCIFER.

THE LIGHT-BEARER.

Third Series Vol. VI., No. [illegible] CHICAGO, ILLINOIS DEC. 11, E. M. 302. [C. E. 1902.] Whole No. 94[illegible]

Free Speech in Chicago

EDITOR LUCIFER:—For the benefit of those of your readers who still believe that freedom of speech is a reality, and that America is the freest country on earth, permit me to give you a few details of my experience with the Chicago police.

I came to this city to acquaint the American public with the conditions in Russia, and to raise funds for the unfortunate victims of the Russian knout, many of whom have been flogged to death, while others have been sent to long terms of imprisonment, simply because they dared to ask for bread for the suffering Russian peasants.

To my amazement I found two hundred policemen—some of them high officials, at my first meeting; men who came not out of sympathy with the starving Russian people but who were there to take me to the nearest police station should I not meet their own conception of what liberty means.

O Liberty! poor outraged, degraded Liberty. Fallen indeed art thou from thy once lofty height when every petty policeman can soil thy pure form with his foul hands, and trample in the mire of Chicago's streets thy beauteous lineaments.

Since that first meeting the police have followed me from hall to hall, threatening me with arrest if I dared to say anything against the American government. "Say what you please about Russia, but you must not attack OUR institutions," said Captain Campbell to me at a meeting on the West side.

Another little Tzar, Captain Wheeler, went his colleague one better: "I will not have Miss Goldman speak in my district." and prohibited the meeting that was to take place at Aurora Turn Hall, corner of Ashland Ave. and Division street.

Surely there must be something wrong with the American Institutions of today; something terribly black and corrupt, if they cannot stand the light of criticism; if they can thrive only when physical force is used to defend them against the light of free discussion.

This is not the first time that meetings for free discussion have been prohibited here; not the first time speakers have been shadowed from place to place. On previous occasions the Chicago authorities have had to give some excuse for such interference. They have had to plead either public excitement, to radical utterance on the part of the speaker, or some similar excuse as justification of their acts.

What excuse will they give now?

What excuse will the self-styled Jeffersonian-Democratic mayor of Chicago give for the acts of his subordinates?

There is now no public excitement; no radical utterance made—at least not in reference to "our own sacred government."

What other conclusion can be reached, or inference drawn than that America is fast being Russianized, and that unless the American people awake from the pleasant dream into what they have been lulled by the strains of "My Country 'tis of Thee," etc., we shall soon be obliged to meet in cellars, or darkened back rooms with closed doors, and speak in whispers lest our next door neighbors should hear that free-born American citizens dare not speak in the open; that they have sold the birthright to the Russian Tzar disguised by the coat of American policeman?

Is it not time that SOMETHING BE DONE?

Is it not time that all advanced people unite in protest against such brutal invasion? all, at least, who have enough Americanism left in them to maintain the right of freedom of speech, of press and of assembly?

Or, are they going to wait until the number of victims of suppression increase to legions—as in Russia today?

Chicago, Nov. 30, 1902. EMMA GOLDMAN.

Document Eleven

Cover of Alden Freeman pamphlet, "The Fight for Free Speech," with excerpt from *New York Times* article, "Goldman Champions Win the East Side," July 1, 1909

Context: As people like Goldman were prevented from speaking, societies formed to protect the right to free speech. A pamphlet created by Alden Freeman alerted people to the fight for free speech. It contains a tongue-in-cheek *New York Times* account of his attempt to hold a meeting where Emma Goldman could speak freely and without police restriction.

Questions on the Document:

Pamphlet cover:

What do the quotations on the cover from Wendell Phillips, Benjamin Franklin, and Thomas Paine say about liberty?

What does this pamphlet say it contains? How might participants in a free speech campaign use this pamphlet?

What arguments might free speech advocates use to support their title, "Law-Breaking by the Police"?

Newspaper article:

Who is Alden Freeman, and what happened to him as a result of inviting Emma Goldman to lecture?

Does Freeman fit your image of a "Mayflower descendant"?

Why was Goldman perceived by some to be a threat even when she was lecturing on modern drama?

What clues do you have that the article is intended to be a humorous account of a secretive meeting of Mayflower descendants and anarchists?

Was speaking in public against the law? Who was responsible for enforcing the law? Why might the official response to Goldman's lectures have been so unpredictable?

General Questions:

Would you stand up for an unpopular view if it meant that you would lose your friends?

How do such groups as Amnesty International, the Sanctuary movement, and other recent human rights movements compare to the free speech movement?

Does the race, gender, ethnicity, and class of the advocate of an unpopular cause affect the reception or rejection of their message?

The manna of liberty must be gathered each day, or it is rotten.

Only by unintermitted agitation can a people be kept sufficiently awake to principle not to let liberty be smothered in material prosperity.

Republics exist only on the tenure of being agitated.

—WENDELL PHILLIPS

THE FIGHT
FOR
FREE SPEECH

A SUPPLEMENT TO

"LAW-BREAKING BY THE POLICE"

Including a Legal Opinion by THEODORE SCHROEDER, Attorney for the Free Speech League.

A list of Free Speech Literature, Striking Incidents of the Campaign, Comments of the Press and General Information for the Use of Workers for Free Speech.

COMPILED

BY

ALDEN FREEMAN

Where liberty dwells, there is my country.

—BENJAMIN FRANKLIN

Where liberty dwells NOT, there is mine.

THOMAS PAINE

GOLDMAN CHAMPIONS WIN THE EAST SIDE.

Alden Freeman Pleads for Free Speech Before a Cooper Union Audience—Very Orderly "Anarchists"—Leonard Dalton Abbott Opens the Meeting—Miss de Cleyre Talks Vigorously—Mrs. Milton Rathbun Makes a Hit—Emma Goldman Not Present.

[Witty Account by CHARLES WILLIS THOMPSON, in NEW YORK TIMES of July 1, 1909]

Spotless Town has been located. It is in East Orange, N. J. Alden Freeman says so, and he lives there and ought to know.

Alden Freeman is the Mayflower descendant who got rousted (Not yet, not on your life!—A. F.) out of a genealogical society or two for inviting Emma Goldman, the Anarchist, to partake of a few mayflowers in East Orange, N. J., on the occasion of some grand celebration or other. He also wrote a letter to Mayor McClellan complaining that the police had made him ill by chasing him and several hundred other American citizens into the street when they had paid good American money to hear Miss Goldman lecture on that incendiary topic, "The Drama."

Last night the most rigidly law-abiding people in the city of New York—we refer, of course, to the Anarchists—got together in Cooper Union to express their indignation over the action of the police in suppressing Emma Goldman every time she tried to talk, and they let Alden Freeman, a Puritan unto the third and fourth generation, preside over them.

It was a funny crowd, viewed from our New York standpoint. Now, normally, you would suppose that a lot of Anarchists would be the most uncontrollable and lawless outfit you would get together. Actually these Anarchists gave any Presbyterian prayer meeting cards and spades on courtesy and decency. If a man tried to get out of there before the meeting was over he sneaked out; he concealed himself; he tried to avoid observation.

It was entirely different from the average Republican or Democratic massmeeting, where as soon as the star speaker has got through everybody rises and makes a sprint for the doorway. And if anybody tried to applaud at the wrong time he was hissed down.

The fuss was over the fact that some time ago, when Emma Goldman went to Harlem and tried to tell an audience that Ibsen had Hauptmann beaten as a dramatist and that Eugene Walter was the hope of the American stage, a lot of policemen chased her off the stage on the theory that Hauptmann was probably an Anarchist because he was Dutch. This outrage had rankled in the minds of the Anarchists, and they had hired Cooper Union for $75 to show that they didn't like it.

Leonard D. Abbott opened the meeting. He is an editor—runs a magazine, in fact. When he got on the platform he confronted the most earnest crowd that has filled Cooper Union in many a day. At the outset they had a line of policemen stationed around the hall, presumably to arrest Emma Goldman if she should get up and erupt some incendiary sentiment such as "Eugene Walter is a great dramatist"—which is about as far as Emma Goldman goes these days.

But Leonard Abbott announced, "right off the bat," that Miss Goldman wasn't going to speak, and wasn't even going to be there, because she would surely be arrested as soon as she opened her mouth, and the promoters of the meeting didn't care for any police interference.

But Leonard Abbott and everybody else who talked last night rubbed in the fact that Miss Goldman would make a speech at 100 West 116th street on Friday—count it: 100 West—near Lenox avenue—take the Subway—you can't miss it.

Excerpt from a New York Times *article reprinted in Alden Freeman's pamphlet with his parenthetical editorial comments.*

Document Twelve
The San Diego Free Speech Incident

a. Excerpt from *Living My Life*

b. IWW logo, "Join the One Big Union"

c. *Mother Earth* cover, "Patriotism in Action," June 1912

**d. *Los Angeles Times* article,
"Reitman, the Tarred Anarchist, Comes In," May 16, 1912**

Context: The Industrial Workers of the World (IWW), a militant labor union that sought to organize all workers regardless of their level of skill into "One Big Union" to foster workers' control of industries, was prevented from organizing in many cities. Local governments passed ordinances denying IWW leaders the right to speak in public places. In San Diego in 1912, the union held a mass public rally to challenge the ordinances. In the first week 150 "Wobblies" (the popular name for members of the IWW) were jailed. Private vigilante groups terrorized IWW members and sympathizers, and drove them out of town. Emma Goldman and her road manager, Ben Reitman, joined the San Diego free speech fight.

Questions on the Document:
Describe the events in the San Diego incident.
Summarize the mayor's position and Goldman's position on her free speech rights in San Diego. How were these viewpoints in conflict with each other?
Did the mayor and town authority behave responsibly in this situation?
What happened to Ben Reitman according to the *Los Angeles Times* report?
What was the reporter's opinion of Reitman, Goldman and the anarchists? How do you know?
How was the San Diego incident portrayed on the cover of *Mother Earth*? What is happening in the drawing? Who are the men? What symbols are used to make a political point? What does the title mean?

General Questions:
Do you think criticism of American government is unpatriotic? Why?
What, in your opinion, are the most controversial issues of the day? Which elicit the most violent responses?
What price might a person pay when they advocate a cause that falls outside of the "mainstream"?
What groups in America's past have used vigilantism to achieve their goals? What groups practice vigilantism in today's society?
When and why do you think groups resort to vigilante activities?

Excerpt from *Living My Life* (volume 1, pp. 494-501)

Vigilante activity in San Diego

When I arrived with Ben [Reitman] in Los Angeles in April [1912], San Diego was in the grip of a veritable civil war. The patriots, known as Vigilantes, had converted the city into a battle-field. They beat, clubbed, and killed men and women who still believed in their constitutional rights. Hundreds of them had come to San Diego from every part of the United States to participate in the campaign. They travelled in box cars, on the bumpers, on the roofs of trains, every moment in danger of their lives, yet sustained by the holy quest for freedom of speech, for which their comrades were already filling the jails.

The Vigilantes raided the I.W.W. headquarters, broke up the furniture, and arrested a large number of men found there. They were taken out to Sorrento to a spot where a flag-pole had been erected. There the I.W.W.'s were forced to kneel, kiss the flag, and sing the national anthem. As an incentive to quicker action one of the Vigilantes would slap them on the back, which was the signal for a general beating. After these proceedings the men were loaded into automobiles and sent to San Onofre, near the county line, placed in a cattle-pen with armed guards over them, and kept without food or drink for eighteen hours. The following morning they were taken out in groups of five and compelled to run the gauntlet. As they passed between the double line of Vigilantes, they were belaboured with clubs and blackjacks. Then the flag-kissing episode was repeated, after which they were told to "hike" up the track and never come back. They reached Los Angeles after a tramp of several days, sore, hungry, penniless, and in deplorable physical condition.

IWW Sticker

In this struggle, in which the local police were on the side of the Vigilantes, several I.W.W. men lost their lives. The most brutal murder was that of Joseph Mikolasek, who died on May 7. He was one of the many rebels who had attempted to fill the gap caused by the arrest of their speakers. When he ascended the platform, he was assaulted by the police. With difficulty he dragged himself to the socialist headquarters, and thence home. He was followed by detectives, who attacked him in his house. One officer fired and severely wounded him. In self-defence Mikolasek had picked up an ax, but his body was riddled with bullets before he had a chance to lift it against his assailants.

On every tour to the Coast I had lectured in San Diego. This time we were also planning meetings there after the close of our Los Angeles engagements. Reports from San Diego and the arrival of scores of wounded Vigilante victims decided us to go at once. Especially after the killing of Mikolasek we felt it imperative to take up the free-speech fight

Excerpt from *Living My Life* (volume 1, pp. 494-501)

I go to lecture in San Diego—

waged there. First, however, it was necessary to organize relief for the destitute boys who had escaped their tormentors and had reached us alive. With the help of a group of women we organized a feeding-station at the I.W.W. headquarters. We raised funds at my meetings and collected clothing and food-stuffs from sympathetic store-keepers.

San Diego was not content with the murder of Mikolasek; it would not permit him even to be buried in the city. We therefore had his body shipped to Los Angeles, and prepared a public demonstration in his honour. Joseph Mikolasek had been obscure and unknown in life, but he grew to country-wide stature in his death. Even the police of the city were impressed by the size, dignity, and grief of the masses that followed his remains to the crematorium.

Some comrades in San Diego had undertaken to arrange a meeting, and I chose a subject which seemed to express the situation best—Henrik Ibsen's *An Enemy of the People*.

On our arrival we found a dense crowd at the station. It did not occur to me that the reception was intended for us; I thought that some State official was being expected. We were to be met by our friends Mr. and Mrs. E. E. Kirk, but they were nowhere to be seen, and Ben suggested that we go to the U.S. Grant Hotel. We passed unobserved and got into the hotel autobus. It was hot and stuffy inside and we climbed up on top. We had barely taken our seats when someone shouted: "Here she is, here's the Goldman woman!" At once the cry was taken up by the crowd. Fashionably dressed women stood up in their cars screaming: "We want that anarchist murderess!" In an instant there was a rush for the autobus, hands reaching up to pull me down. With unusual presence of mind, the chauffeur started the car at full speed, scattering the crowd in all directions.

At the hotel we met with no objections. We registered and were shown to our rooms. Everything seemed normal. Mr. and Mrs. Kirk called to see us, and we quietly discussed final arrangements for our meeting. In the afternoon the head clerk came to announce that the Vigilantes had insisted on looking over the hotel register to secure the number of our rooms; he would therefore have to transfer us to another part of the house. We were taken on the top floor and assigned to a large suite. Later on, Mr. Holmes, the hotel manager, paid us a visit. We were perfectly safe under his roof, he assured us, but he could not permit us to go down for our meals or leave our rooms. He would have to keep us locked in. I protested that the U.S. Grant Hotel was not a prison. He replied that he could not keep us incarcerated against our will, but that, as long as we remained the guests of the house, we should have to submit to his arrangement for our safety. "The Vigilantes are in an ugly mood," he warned us; "they are determined not to let you speak and to drive you both out of town." He urged us to leave of our own account and volunteered to escort us. He was a kindly man and we appreciated his offer, but we had to refuse it.

Mr. Holmes had barely left when I was called on the telephone. The speaker said that his name was Edwards, that he was at the head of the local Conservatory of Music, and that he had just read in the papers that our hall-keeper had backed out. He offered us the recital hall of the conservatory. "San Diego still seems to have some brave men," I said to the

—and am warmly greeted on my arrival

mysterious person at the other end of the telephone, and I invited him to come to see me to talk over his plan. Before long a fine-looking man of about twenty-seven called. In the course of our conversation I pointed out to him that I might cause him trouble by speaking in his place. He replied that he did not mind; he was an anarchist in art and he believed in free speech. If I were willing to take a chance, so was he. We decided to await developments.

Towards evening a bedlam of auto horns and whistles filled the street. "The Vigilantes!" Ben cried. There was a knock at the door, and Mr. Holmes came in, accompanied by two other men. I was wanted downstairs by the city authorities, they informed me. Ben sensed danger and insisted that I ask them to send the visitors up. It seemed timid to me. It was early evening and we were in the principal hotel of the city. What could happen to us? I went with Mr. Holmes, Ben accompanying us. Downstairs we were ushered into a room where we found seven men standing in a semicircle. We were asked to sit down and wait for the Chief of Police, who arrived before long. "Please come with me," he addressed me; "the Mayor and other officials are awaiting you next door." We got up to follow, but, turning to Ben, the Chief said: "You are not wanted, doctor. Better wait here."

I entered a room filled with men. The window-blinds were partly drawn, but the large electric street light in front disclosed an agitated mass below. The Mayor approached me. "You hear that mob," he said, indicating the street; "they mean business. They want to get you and Reitman out of the hotel, even if they have to take you by force. We cannot guarantee anything. If you consent to leave, we will give you protection and get you safely out of town."

"That's very nice of you," I replied, "but why don't you disperse the crowd? Why don't you use the same measures against these people that you have against the free-speech fighters? Your ordinance makes it a crime to gather in the business districts. Hundreds of I.W.W.'s, anarchists, socialists, and trade-union men have been clubbed and arrested, and some even killed, for this offence. Yet you allow the Vigilante mob to congregate in the busiest part of the town and obstruct traffic. All you have to do is to disperse these law-breakers."

"We can't do it," he said abruptly; "These people are in a dangerous mood, and your presence makes things worse."

"Very well, then, let me speak to the crowd," I suggested. "I could do it from a window here. I have faced infuriated men before and I have always been able to pacify them."

The Mayor refused.

"I have never accepted protection from the police," I then said, "and I do not intend to do so now. I charge all of you men here with being in league with the Vigilantes."

"Thereupon the officials declared that matters would have to take their course, and that I should have only myself to blame if anything happened.

The interview at an end, I went to call Ben. The room I had left him in was locked. I became alarmed and pounded on the door. There was no answer. The noise I made brought a hotel clerk. He unlocked the door, but no one was there. I ran back to the other room and met the Chief, who was just coming out.

Excerpt from *Living My Life* (volume 1, pp. 494-501)

Ben is abducted

"Where is Reitman?" I demanded. "What have you done with him? If any harm comes to him, you will pay for it if I have to do it with my own hands."

"How should I know?" he replied gruffly.

Mr. Holmes was not in his office, and no one would tell me what had become of Ben Reitman. In consternation I returned to my room. Ben did not appear. In dismay I paced the floor, unable to decide what steps to take or whom to approach to help me find Ben. I could not call any person I knew in the city without endangering his safety, least of all Mr. Kirk; he was already under indictment in connexion with the free-speech fight. It had been brave of him and his wife to meet us; it was sure to aggravate his situation. The circumstance that the Kirks did not return as they had promised proved that they were being kept away.

I felt helpless. Time dragged on, and at midnight I dozed off from sheer fatigue. I dreamed of Ben, bound and gagged, his hands groping for me. I struggled to reach him and woke up with a scream, bathed in sweat. There were voices and loud knocking at my door. When I opened, the house detective and another man stepped in. Reitman was safe, they told me. I looked at them in a daze, hardly grasping their meaning. Ben had been taken out by the Vigilantes, they explained, but no harm had come to him. They had only put him on a train for Los Angeles. I did not believe the detective, but the other man looked honest. He reiterated that he had been given absolute assurance that Reitman was safe.

Mr. Holmes came in. He corroborated the man and begged me to consent to leave. There was no object in my remaining any longer in town, he urged. I would not be allowed to lecture and I was only endangering his own position. He hoped I would not take undue advantage because I was a woman. If I remained, the Vigilantes would drive me out of town anyhow.

Mr. Holmes seemed genuinely concerned. I knew there was no chance of holding a meeting. Now that Ben was safe, there was no sense in harassing Mr. Holmes any further. I consented to leave, planning to take the Owl, the 2:45 A.M train, for Los Angeles. I called for a taxi and drove to the station. The town was asleep, the streets deserted.

I had just purchased my ticket and was walking towards the Pullman car when I caught the sound of approaching autos—the fearful sound I had first heard at the station and later at the hotel. The Vigilantes, of course.

"Hurry, hurry!" someone cried; "get in quick!"

Before I had time to make another step, I was picked up, carried to the train, and literally thrown into the compartment. The blinds were pulled down and I was locked in. The Vigilantes had arrived and were rushing up and down the platform, shouting and trying to board the train. The crew was on guard, refusing to let them on. There was mad yelling and cursing—hideous and terrifying moments till at last the train pulled out.

We stopped at innumerable stations. Each time I peered out eagerly in the hope that Ben might be waiting to join me. But there was no sign of him. When I reached my apartment in Los Angeles, he was not there. The U.S. Grant Hotel men had lied in order to get me out of town! . . .

Excerpt from *Living My Life* (volume 1, pp. 494-501)

Ben relates details of his torture

At ten o'clock I was called on the long-distance phone. A strange voice informed me that Dr. Reitman was boarding the train for Los Angeles and that he would arrive in the late afternoon. "His friends should bring a stretcher to the station." "Is he alive?" I shouted into the receiver. "Are you telling the truth? Is he alive?" I listened breathlessly, but there was no response.

The hours dragged on as if the day would never pass. The wait at the station was more excruciating still. At last the train pulled in. Ben lay in a rear car, all huddled up. He was in blue overalls, his face deathly pale, a terrified look in his eyes. His hat was gone, and his hair was sticky with tar. At the sight of me he cried: "Oh, Mommy, I'm with you at last! Take me away, take me home!"

The newspaper men besieged him with questions, but he was too exhausted to speak. I begged them to leave him alone and to call later at my apartment.

While helping him to undress, I was horrified to see that his body was a mass of bruises covered with blotches of tar. The letters I.W.W. were burned into his flesh. Ben could not speak; only his eyes tried to convey what he had passed through. After partaking of some nourishment and sleeping several hours, he regained a little strength. In the presence of a number of friends and reporters he told us what had happened to him.

"When Emma and the hotel manager left the office to go into another room," Ben related, "I remained alone with seven men. As soon as the door was closed, they drew out revolvers. 'If you utter a sound or make a move, we'll kill you,' they threatened. Then they gathered around me. One man grabbed my right arm, another the left; a third took hold of the front of my coat, another of the back, and I was led out into the corridor, down the elevator to the ground floor of the hotel, and out into the street past a uniformed policeman, and then thrown into an automobile. When the mob saw me, they set up a howl. The auto went slowly down the main street and was joined by another one containing several persons who looked like business men. This was about half past ten in the evening. The twenty-mile ride was frightful. As soon as we got out of town, they began kicking and beating me. They took turns at pulling my long hair and they stuck their fingers into my eyes and nose. 'We could tear your guts out,' they said, 'but we promised the Chief of Police not to kill you. We are responsible men, property-owners, and the police are on our

Ben's case arouses nation-wide indignation

side.' When we reached the county line, the auto stopped at a deserted spot. The men formed a ring and told me to undress. They tore my clothes off. They knocked me down, and when I lay naked on the ground, they kicked and beat me until I was almost insensible. With a lighted cigar they burned the letters I.W.W. on my buttocks; then they poured a can of tar over my head and, in the absence of feathers, rubbed sage-brush on my body. One of them attempted to push a cane into my rectum. Another twisted my testicles. They forced me to kiss the flag and sing *The Star Spangled Banner*. When they tired of the fun, they gave me my underwear for fear we should meet any women. They also gave me back my vest, in order that I might carry my money, railroad ticket, and watch. The rest of my clothes they kept. I was ordered to make a speech, and then they commanded me to run the gauntlet. The Vigilantes lined up, and as I ran past them, each one gave me a blow or a kick. Then they let me go."

State and Coast. Part II—The City and
The Los Angeles Times
Population:
THURSDAY MORNING, MAY 16, 1912. 16 PAGES. PRICE:

Gang Welcomes Him.

REITMAN, THE TARRED ANARCHIST, COMES IN.

DECKED in a newly-purchased outfit suggesting a Mexican peon, and with traces of tar still clinging to his seared features, Dr. Ben Reitman, the anarchist, arrived in the city last night fresh from the hands of San Diego vigilantes. That his experience with aroused public sentiment was not pleasant was indicated by his forlorn appearance, as he got off a Santa Fe train at 6:30 o'clock.

A large following of anarchists and other undesirable human parasites congregated at the station to welcome the crestfallen leader, but the anarchists were cowed by the show of force and determination of the police under personal command of Capt. Murray. As soon as the train arrived the crowd of sympathizers made a rush, but were held in check by the police, and as Reitman pressed forward the crowd was kept moving without allowing the members time to start trouble had they been so inclined.

The Goldman woman was among the first to welcome Reitman, when his identity had been established. He was not at first recognized in his blue overalls and black slouch hat, which he had found it necessary to buy in lieu of his ordinary street apparel. His face was covered with deep burns, showing that the hot tar applied by the angry vigilantes had forever marked the man.

As Reitman and his followers were slowly pressed toward the street, a representative of an evening socialistic sheet came forward and after giving the high sign was welcomed as a brother by the I.W.W. bosses. At his suggestion the party entered an automobile provided by the management of the paper and was driven to the Hotel Antlers, where Miss Goldman had taken rooms upon her arrival from San Diego early yesterday morning.

"Upon being taken from the Hotel Grant in San Diego I sought refuge in a Pullman sleeper," said Miss Goldman. "I had been in the car but a short time when another mob formed outside and for a time I believed my life in danger. I now know that the men were looking for my manager for the purpose of heaping indignities upon him."

Reitman declared himself physically exhausted and unable to say anything except that he is not discouraged and will continue his propaganda while life lasts. One of the anarchist leaders volunteered the information that Reitman had not only been tarred and feathered, but had been branded with the letters "I.W.W." by means of a lighted cigar.

After having been turned loose by the vigilantes, Reitman walked to Oceanside, where he spent yesterday rolling in the sand and surf in an effort to remove the tar and other crudities. He succeeded, and as he was anxious to join his companions in this city it was decided to buy the cheap jumper and overalls.

Document Thirteen
Meeting with Lenin, 1920

a. Excerpt from *My Disillusionment in Russia* by Emma Goldman (1923)

b. Photograph of Lenin

c. Questions presented to Lenin by Goldman and Berkman

Context: After Emma Goldman's deportation in 1919 from the United States, she arrived in Soviet Russia hoping she "would find a new-born country, with its people wholly consecrated to the great task of revolutionary reconstruction." Goldman soon realized that her view of the Revolution was not shared by the Bolshevik leadership. In this "new" Russia, anarchists and other activists were denied free speech, and their organizing efforts landed them in jail. In a meeting with Lenin arranged by her friend Angelica Balabanova, a trusted advisor of Lenin, Goldman protested their treatment. Disillusioned and convinced that Lenin had betrayed the ideals of the Revolution, after fifteen months Goldman left Soviet Russia.

Questions on the Document:s
What did Emma Goldman expect to work out with the Soviet government?
Why was an interview with Lenin important for Goldman?
Why do you think Lenin granted Goldman an interview?
What were Lenin's views on free speech? Why did he feel that way?

General Questions:
How important is the right to free speech in a society where a struggle for the economic basics of life is the first priority?
What reputation does Lenin have in the former Soviet Union?
Name recent incidents around the world where movements for free speech have developed. What were the outcomes?

Excerpt from *My Disillusionment in Russia* by Emma Goldman

Chapter V
MEETING PEOPLE

At a conference of the Moscow Anarchists in March I first learned of the part some Anarchists had played in the Russian Revolution. In the July uprising of 1917 the Kronstadt sailors were led by the Anarchist Yarchuck;...the Anarchists had participated on every front and helped to drive back the Allied attacks. It was the consensus of opinion that the Anarchists were always among the first to face fire, as they were also the most active in the reconstructive work. One of the biggets factories near Moscow, which did not stop work during the entire period of the Revolution, was managed by an Anarchist. Anarchists were doing important work in the Foreign Office and in all other departments. I learned that the Anarchists had virtually helped the Bolsheviki into power. Five months later, in April, 1918, machine guns were used to destroy the Moscow Anarchist Club and to suppress their Press. ... The field had to be "cleared of disturbing elements," and the Anarchists were the first to suffer. Since then the persecution of the Anarchists has never ceased.

Lenin in his study in the Kremlin, 1918

The Moscow Anarchist Conference was critical not only toward the existing régime, but toward its own comrades as well. It spoke frankly of the negative sides of the movement, and of its lack of unity and coöperation during the revolutionary period. Later I was to learn more of the internal dissensions in the Anarchist movement. Before closing, the Conference decided to call on the Soviet Government to release the imprisoned Anarchists and to legalize Anarchist educational work. The Conference asked Alexander Berkman and myself to sign the resolution to that effect. It was a shock to me that Anarchists should ask any government to legalize their efforts, but I still believed the Soviet Government to be at least to some extent expressive of the Revolution. I signed the resolution, and as I was to see Lenin in a few days I promised to take the matter up with him.

The interview with Lenin was arranged by Balabanova. "You must see Ilitch, talk to him about the things that are disturbing you and the work you would like to do," she had said. But some time passed before the opportunity came. At last one day Balabanova called up to ask whether I could go at once. Lenin had sent his car and we were quickly driven over to the Kremlin, passed without

Excerpt from *My Disillusionment in Russia* by Emma Goldman

question by the guards, and at last ushered into the workroom of the all-powerful president of the People's Commissars.

When we entered Lenin held a copy of the brochure *Trial and Speeches** in his hands. I had given my only copy to Balabanova, who had evidently sent the booklet on ahead of us to Lenin. One of his first questions was, "When could the Social Revolution be expected in America?" I had been asked the question repeatedly before, but I was astounded to hear it from Lenin. It seemed incredible that a man of his information should know so little about conditions in America. ...

I broached the subject of the Anarchists in Russia. I showed him a letter I had received from Martens, the Soviet representative in America, shortly before my deportation. Martens asserted that the Anarchists in Russia enjoyed full freedom of speech and Press. Since my arrival I found scores of Anarchists in prison and their Press suppressed. I explained that I could not think of working with the Soviet Government so long as my comrades were in prison for opinion's sake. I also told him of the resolutions of the Moscow Anarchist Conference. He listened patiently and promised to bring the matter to the attention of his party. "But as to free speech," he remarked, "that is, of course, a bourgeois notion. There can be no free speech in a revolutionary period. We have the peasantry against us because we can give them nothing in return for their bread. We will have them on our side when we have something to exchange. Then you can have all the free speech you want—but not now. Recently we needed peasants to cart some wood into the city. They demanded salt. We thought we had no salt, but then we discovered seventy poods in Moscow in one of our warehouses. At once the peasants were willing to cart the wood. Your comrades must wait until we can meet the needs of the peasants. Meanwhile, they should work with us. ..."

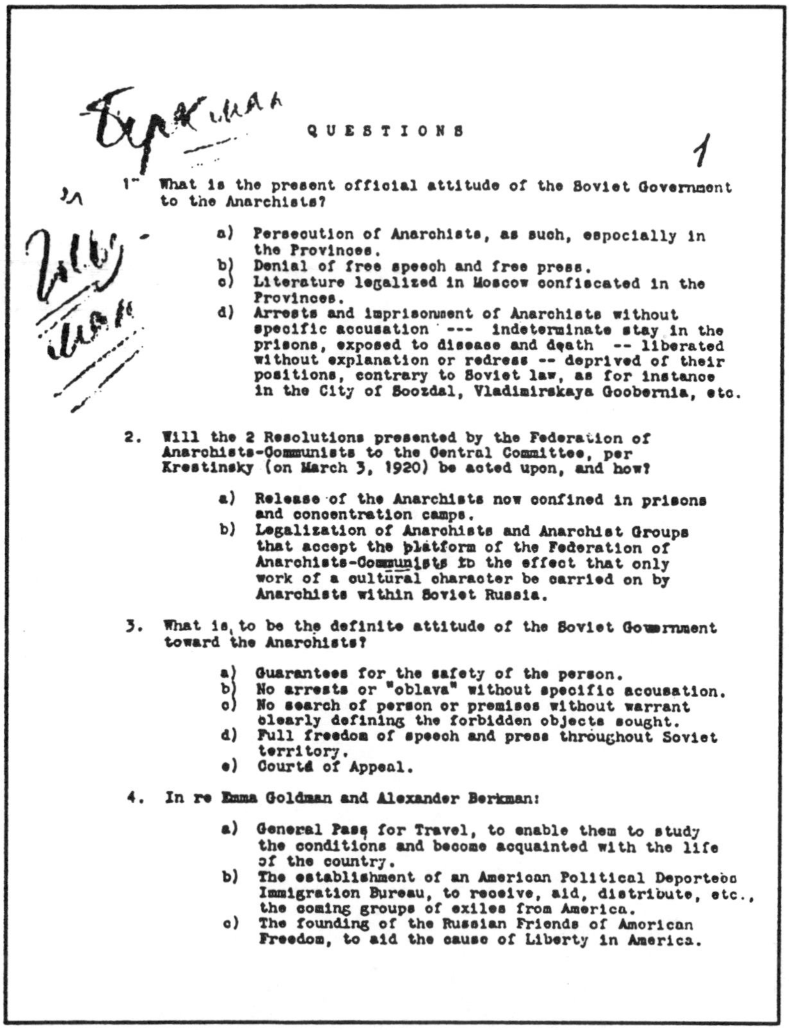

QUESTIONS

1. What is the present official attitude of the Soviet Government to the Anarchists?

   a) Persecution of Anarchists, as such, especially in the Provinces.
   b) Denial of free speech and free press.
   c) Literature legalized in Moscow confiscated in the Provinces.
   d) Arrests and imprisonment of Anarchists without specific accusation --- indeterminate stay in the prisons, exposed to disease and death -- liberated without explanation or redress -- deprived of their positions, contrary to Soviet law, as for instance in the City of Soozdal, Vladimirskaya Goobernia, etc.

2. Will the 2 Resolutions presented by the Federation of Anarchists-Communists to the Central Committee, per Krestinsky (on March 3, 1920) be acted upon, and how?

   a) Release of the Anarchists now confined in prisons and concentration camps.
   b) Legalization of Anarchists and Anarchist Groups that accept the platform of the Federation of Anarchists-Communists to the effect that only work of a cultural character be carried on by Anarchists within Soviet Russia.

3. What is to be the definite attitude of the Soviet Government toward the Anarchists?

   a) Guarantees for the safety of the person.
   b) No arrests or "oblava" without specific accusation.
   c) No search of person or premises without warrant clearly defining the forbidden objects sought.
   d) Full freedom of speech and press throughout Soviet territory.
   e) Courts of Appeal.

4. In re Emma Goldman and Alexander Berkman:

   a) General Pass for Travel, to enable them to study the conditions and become acquainted with the life of the country.
   b) The establishment of an American Political Deportees Immigration Bureau, to receive, aid, distribute, etc., the coming groups of exiles from America.
   c) The founding of the Russian Friends of American Freedom, to aid the cause of Liberty in America.

Questions presented to Lenin in 1920 by Goldman and Berkman about the persecution of anarchists. (Central Party Archives of the Institute of Marxism-Leninism, Moscow)

Free speech, free Press, the spiritual achievements of centuries, what were they to this man? A Puritan, he was sure his scheme alone could redeem Russia. Those who served his plans were right, the others could not be tolerated.

**Trial and Speeches of Alexander Berkman and Emma Goldman before the Federal Court of New York, June-July*, 1917, Mother Earth Publishing Co., New York.

Topic Two: Freedom of Expression
Suggested Activities

Read the First Amendment. In your own words, what does it mean?

Find contemporary political cartoons or create your own that portray a group using direct action as a political tactic. After seeing such cartoons are you more or less sympathetic to the group? If you were drawing a cartoon of this group would you make any changes in the cartoon?

See what your textbook says about *anarchism.* Is this definition similar to or different from descriptions of anarchism found in these documents? Find out about Henry David Thoreau, Ralph Waldo Emerson, Thomas Jefferson, and John Brown. Relate their thoughts and actions to the philosophy of anarchism.

Locate contemporary images that illustrate the concept, "freedom of expression." For example, posters, magazine ads, cartoons. Discuss your findings in class. Draw an illustration of your own.

Analyze at least two editorials on any topic. Do you think these opinions are objective? Why or why not? Use these examples as models for writing your own editorial on a topic that interests you.

Find newspaper articles that address the question of free speech today. Debate the opposing positions presented by the press.

Divide students into groups. One group reviews the documents for arguments in favor of unlimited free speech; the other for arguments for limitations on free speech. Then, in debating team format, discuss the issues.

Choose a document on any topic in this section to compare and contrast opposing views (i.e., Lenin's view of free speech vs. the view held by Alexander Berkman and Emma Goldman). Identify the bias in each.

Identify times and places in American history when free speech was at issue: for example, opposition to America's involvement in war; the abolitionist movement; birth control; Berkeley free speech movement; Nazi parade in Skokie, Illinois; Lenny Bruce; consumer warning labels on music recordings; rap musicians; the Industrial Workers of the World (IWW), the Ku Klux Klan, communists. What were the circumstances surrounding the incidents? What similarities appear in these examples? What differences?

Create a dramatic reading of the San Diego incident.

Research the following Supreme Court decisions on free speech: Alien and Sedition Acts **(1798)**; Schenck v. U.S. **(1919)**; Tinker v. Des Moines Community School District **(1969)**; Bethel School District No. 403 v. Fraser, 478 U.S. 675 **(1986)**; Hazelwood School District v. Kuhlmeier, 484 U.S. 260 **(1988)**.

(continued, next page)

Topic Two Suggested Activities, continued

Conduct a mock trial based on the Supreme Court decisions (Tinker, Fraser, and Hazelwood as cited above) on which the following scenarios are based:

a. Students in a public high school wear black arm bands to class to protest the United States' involvement in the Gulf War. The school board orders the students to remove the bands or be expelled. Is the right of the students to wear arm bands protected by the First Amendment?

b. A high school senior was suspended for delivering a nomination speech that included an explicit sexual term to describe his candidate. The senior was suspended. He argued that his speech caused no disruption and was protected by the First Amendment. Was the student's suspension an abuse of his First Amendment rights?

c. A high school principal censored articles in the school paper dealing with the effects of divorce on students and with student pregnancies on the grounds that he was obliged to protect their privacy. The student editors claimed the principal violated their First Amendment rights of freedom of the press. Was the principal's decision in violation of the First Amendment?

TOPIC THREE

Women's Rights

TOPIC THREE: Women's Rights

Views on women's rights are examined in these documents, revealing both Emma Goldman's public statements and her personal experience in attempting to live out her ideals. They include:

- Marriage—as experienced in the late nineteenth and early twentieth centuries and the particular limits it imposed on women.
- Motherhood—defining parental roles and social responsibility for childrearing.
- Love—definitions of the emotion of love, the nature of jealousy.
- Sexuality—the fight for birth control information, interest in free love outside of marriage, acceptance of varieties of sexual preference.
- Suffrage—a critique of the limited potential of women's voting rights as a means of attaining power.
- Women in the public sphere—attempts to expand women's opportunities outside the home.

Background to the documents: In turn-of-the-century America, Emma Goldman raised "the sex question" in public lectures and debates. She advocated a vision of love as liberating, transforming, and free. Through newspaper interviews, private letters, speeches, and a striking photograph, students will learn how Goldman's commitment to the concept of freedom for the individual applied to women. Documents Fourteen and Fifteen present Goldman's view that marriage inhibits rather than enhances love and creates jealousy.

In a period in which it was unlawful to speak about birth control, Goldman was one of its first public advocates. Documents Sixteen and Seventeen illustrate Goldman's assertion that women have a right to control their bodies. Like Margaret Sanger, Goldman was arrested for speaking out on this issue. She utilized the publicity about the harsh response of the authorities in suppressing her talks to focus attention on the movement. The final document, on women's suffrage, reveals her opinion that the campaign for the vote was basically a middle-class movement limited in its scope and a strategy neither for true liberation nor for the purification of the current political system.

Document Fourteen

Interview with Emma Goldman, "What is There in Anarchy for Woman?" *St. Louis Post-Dispatch*, October 24, 1897

Context: This 1897 interview given to the *St. Louis Post-Dispatch* illustrates Goldman's ideas on love and marriage. She identified with the new ideas about free love that were circulating. For believers in free love, female sexual satisfaction, inside and outside of marriage, was considered natural and desirable. Goldman's willingness to voice "the unspeakable" stimulated both shock and fascination in mainstream America, as evident in the steady stream of front-page newspaper coverage she received.

Questions on the document:
Why did Goldman see marriage as a repressive institution for women? for men?
What aspects of the institution of marriage would be problematic for an anarchist?
What did the reporter think about Goldman?
What were Goldman's feelings about monogamy (loving one person exclusively)?
Did she think that women could have a home and family and still be free?
How would children be raised if Goldman's vision of anarchism became a reality?
Do you think Goldman's definition of love is at its basis "selfish" or "selfless"?

General Questions:
Do you agree or disagree with Goldman's assertion that: "No one can control the affections, therefore there should be no jealousies."
Is there such a thing as equality in marriage? In your opinion, what ingredients are needed to create an equal marriage?
Discuss your thoughts on these or other contemporary issues of love and marriage: domestic partnerships, palimony suits, divorce rates, child custody, non-marital sex.

SUNDAY POST-DISPATCH, MAGAZINE

PART TWO. SUNDAY MORNING—ST. LOUIS—OCTOBER 24, 1897. PAGES 9—16.

WHAT IS THERE IN ANARCHY FOR WOMAN?

—BY EMMA GOLDMAN.—

"WHAT does anarchy hold out to me—a woman?"

"More to woman than to anyone else—everything which she has not—freedom and equality."

Quickly, earnestly Emma Goldman, the priestess of anarchy, exiled from Russia, feared by police, and now a guest of St. Louis Anarchists, gave this answer to my question.

I found her at No. 1722 Oregon avenue, an old-style two-story brick house, the home of a sympathizer—not a relative as has been stated.

I was received by a good-natured, portly German woman, and taken back to a typical German dining-room—everything clean and neat as soap and water could make them. After carefully dusting a chair for me with her apron, she took my name back to the bold little free-thinker. I was welcome. I found Emma Goldman sipping her coffee and partaking of bread and jelly, as her morning's repast. She was neatly clad in a percale shirt waist and skirt, with white collar and cuffs, her feet encased in a loose pair of cloth slippers. She doesn't look like a Russian Nihilist who will be sent to Siberia if she ever crosses the frontier of her native land.

"Do you believe in marriage?" I asked.

"I do not," answered the fair little Anarchist, as promptly as before. I believe that when two people love each other that no judge, minister or court, or body of people, have anything to do with it. They themselves are the ones to determine the relations which they shall hold with one another. When that relation becomes irksome to either party, or one of the parties, then it can be as quietly terminated as it was formed."

From photographs taken by the Sunday *Post-Dispatch* photographer for whom Miss Goldman posed.

Miss Goldman gave a little nod of her head to emphasize her words, and quite a pretty head it was, crowned with soft brown hair, combed with a bang and brushed to one side. Her eyes are the honest blue, her complexion clear and white. Her nose tough rather broad and of a Teutonic type, was well formed. She is short of stature, with a well-rounded figure. Her whole type is more German than Russian. The only serious physical failing that she has is in her eyes. She is so extremely near-sighted that with glasses she can scarcely distinguish print.

"The alliance should be formed," she continued, "not as it is now, to give the woman a support and home, but because the love is there, and that state of affairs can only be brought about by an internal revolution, in short, Anarchy."

She said this as calmly as though she had just expressed an ordinary every-day fact, but the glitter in her eyes showed the "internal revolutions" already at work in her busy brain.

"What does Anarchy promise woman?"

"It holds everything for woman—freedom, equality—everything that woman has not now."

"Isn't woman free?"

"Free! She is the slave of her husband and her children. She should take her part in the business world the same as the man; she should be his equal before the world, as she is in the reality. She is as capable as he, but when she labors she gets less wages. Why? Because she wears skirts instead of trousers."

"But what is to become of the ideal home life, and all that now surrounds the mother, according to a man's idea?"

"Ideal home life, indeed! The woman, instead of being the household queen, told about in story books, is the servant, the mistress, and the slave of both husband and children. She loses her own individuality entirely, even her name she is not allowed to keep. She is the mistress of John Brown or the mistress of Tom Jones; she is that and nothing else. That is the way I think of her."

Miss Goldman has a pleasant accent. She rolls her r's and changes her r's into v's and vice-versa, with a truly Russian pronunciation. She gesticulates a great deal. When she becomes excited her hands and feet and shoulders all help to illustrate her meanings.

"What would you do with the children of the Anarchistic era?"

"The children would be provided with common homes, big boarding schools, where they will be properly cared for and educated and in every way given as good, and in most cases better, care than they would receive in their own homes. Very few mothers know how to take proper care of their children, anyway. It is a science only a very few have learned."

"But the women that desire a home life and the care of their own children, the domestic woman, what of her?"

"Oh, of course, the women that desire could keep their children home and confine themselves as strictly to domestic duties as they desired. But it would give those women who desire something broader, a chance to attain any height they desired. With no poor, and no capitalists, and one common purse, this earth will afford the heaven that the Christians are looking for in another world."

She gazed contemplatively in the bottom of the empty coffee cup, as though she saw in imagination the ideal State, already an actuality.

"Who will take care of the children?" I asked, breaking in upon her reverie.

"Every one," she answered, "has tastes and qualifications suiting them to some occupation. I am a trained nurse. I like to care for the sick. So it will be with some women. They will want to care for and teach the children.

"Won't the children lose their love for their parents and feel the lack of their companionship?" A thought of the affectionate little darlings being relegated to a sort of an orphan asylum crossed my mind.

"The parents will have the same opportunities of gaining their confidences and affections as they have now. They can spend just as much time there as they please or have them with them just as often as desired. They will be the children of love—healthy, strong-minded—and not as now, in most cases, born of hate and domestic dissensions."

"What do you call love?"

"When a man or woman finds some quality or qualities in another that they admire and has an overweening desire to please that person, even to the sacrificing of personal feeling; when there is that subtle something drawing them together, that those who love recognize, and feel it in the inmost fiber of their being, then I call that love." She finished speaking and her face was suffused with a rosy blush.

"Can a person love more than one at a time?"

"I don't see why not—if they find the same lovable qualities in several persons. What should prevent one loving the same things in all of them?

"If we cease to love the man or woman and find some one else, as I said before, we talk it over together and quietly change the mode of living. The private affairs of the family need not then be talked over in the courts and become public property. No one can control the affections, therefore there should be no jealousies.

"Heartaches? Oh, yes," she said, sadly, "but not hatred because he or she has tired of the relations. The human race will always have heartaches as long as the heart beats in the breast.

"My religion," she laughingly repeated. "I was of the Hebrew faith when a girl—you know I am a Jewess—but now I am an atheist. No one has been able to prove either the inspiration of the Bible or the existence of a God to my satisfaction. I believe in no hereafter except the hereafter that is found by the physical matter existing in the human body. I think that lives again in some other form, and I don't think that anything once created over is lost—it goes on and on in first once shape, then another. There is no such thing as a soul—it is all the physical matter."

Pretty Miss Goldman finished speaking, and a delicate flush mounted to her cheek as I asked her if she intended to marry.

"No; I don't believe in marriage for others, and I certainly should not preach one thing and practice another."

She sat in an easy attitude with one leg crossed over the other. She is in every sense a womanly looking woman, with masculine mind and courage.

She laughed as she said there were fifty police at her lecture on Wednesday night, and she added, "If there had of been a bomb thrown I would surely have been blamed for it."

Document Fifteen

a. Excerpt from Goldman's Lecture, "Jealousy—Its Cause and Possible Cure" (1915)

b. 1915 handbill advertising Goldman lecture series

c. Excerpts from Goldman's personal letters to Ben Reitman

d. Photograph of Ben Reitman

Context: Ben Reitman was Emma Goldman's lover and manager. Her intense, passionate attraction to Ben, who had many affairs, made her jealous. Her jealousy conflicted with her belief in free love. Unable to live up to her belief, she said "I have no right to speak of Freedom when I myself have become an abject slave in my love."

Questions on the document:

Do you agree with Goldman that jealousy is not "inborn"? Is it a feeling people can "cure"?

Do you agree with Goldman that males and females become jealous for different reasons?

What emotions does Emma express in her letters to Ben? How do these emotions conflict with her belief in free love?

What specific words from the letters illustrate how Goldman's feelings of jealousy affected her self-image?

Goldman once wrote, "the world would stand aghast that I, Emma Goldman, the strong revolutionist,... the one who has defied laws and convention, should have been as helpless as a shipwrecked crew on a foaming ocean." On the issue of love, why do you think she hid her private agony from her audience?

General Questions:

Goldman discusses the issue of jealousy in love relationships. How would you describe how jealousy arises in friendships, families, and at school?

How can the private letters of a public figure contribute to a more complete understanding of that person?

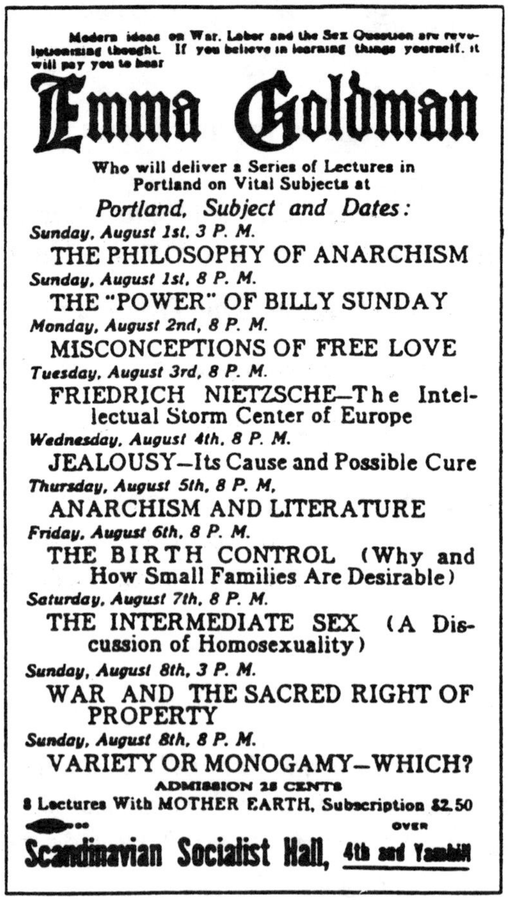

Modern ideas on War, Labor and the Sex Question are revolutionizing thought. If you believe in learning things yourself, it will pay you to hear

Emma Goldman

Who will deliver a Series of Lectures in Portland on Vital Subjects at

Portland, Subject and Dates:

Sunday, August 1st, 3 P. M.
THE PHILOSOPHY OF ANARCHISM

Sunday, August 1st, 8 P. M.
THE "POWER" OF BILLY SUNDAY

Monday, August 2nd, 8 P. M.
MISCONCEPTIONS OF FREE LOVE

Tuesday, August 3rd, 8 P. M.
FRIEDRICH NIETZSCHE—The Intellectual Storm Center of Europe

Wednesday, August 4th, 8 P. M.
JEALOUSY—Its Cause and Possible Cure

Thursday, August 5th, 8 P. M.
ANARCHISM AND LITERATURE

Friday, August 6th, 8 P. M.
THE BIRTH CONTROL (Why and How Small Families Are Desirable)

Saturday, August 7th, 8 P. M.
THE INTERMEDIATE SEX (A Discussion of Homosexuality)

Sunday, August 8th, 3 P. M.
WAR AND THE SACRED RIGHT OF PROPERTY

Sunday, August 8th, 8 P. M.
VARIETY OR MONOGAMY—WHICH?

ADMISSION 25 CENTS

8 Lectures With MOTHER EARTH, Subscription $2.50

OVER

Scandinavian Socialist Hall, 4th and Yamhill

1915 handbill (Holzwarth Collection, University of California, Santa Barbara)

Jealousy—Its Cause and Possible Cure

The most prevalent evil of our mutilated love-life is jealousy, often described as the "green-eyed monster" who lies, cheats, betrays, and kills. The popular notion is that jealousy is inborn and therefore can never be eradicated from the human heart. This idea is a convenient excuse for those who lack ability and willingness to delve into cause and effect....

There are other factors in jealousy: the conceit of the male and the envy of the female. The male in matters sexual is an imposter, a braggart, who forever boasts of his exploits and success with women. He insists on playing the part of a conqueror, since he has been told that women want to be conquered, that they love to be seduced. Feeling himself the only cock in the barnyard....he feels mortally wounded in his conceit and arrogance the moment a rival appears on the scene—the scene, even among so-called refined men, continues to be woman's sex love, which must belong to only one master....

In the case of woman, economic fear for herself and children and her petty envy of every other woman who gains grace in the eyes of her supporter invariably create jealousy. In justice to woman be it said that for centuries past, physical attraction was her only stock in trade, therefore she must needs become envious of the charm and value of other women as threatening her hold upon her precious property.

I hold that every man and woman can help to cure jealousy. The first step towards this is a recognition that they are neither the owners nor controllers nor dictators over the sex functions of the wife or the husband....Whatever we attempt to hold by force, by jealous threats or scenes, through spying and snooping, through mean tricks and soul tortures, is not worth keeping....

Jealousy is indeed a poor medium to secure love, but it is a secure medium to destroy one's self-respect. For jealous people, like dope-fiends, stoop to the lowest level and in the end inspire only disgust and loathing....

All lovers do well to leave the doors of their love wide open. When love can go and come without fear of meeting a watch-dog, jealousy will rarely take root because it will soon learn that where there are no locks and keys there is no place for suspicion and distrust, two elements upon which jealousy thrives and prospers.

Excerpted from a draft of Goldman's lecture "Jealousy—Its Cause and Possible Cure" housed at the New York Public Library.

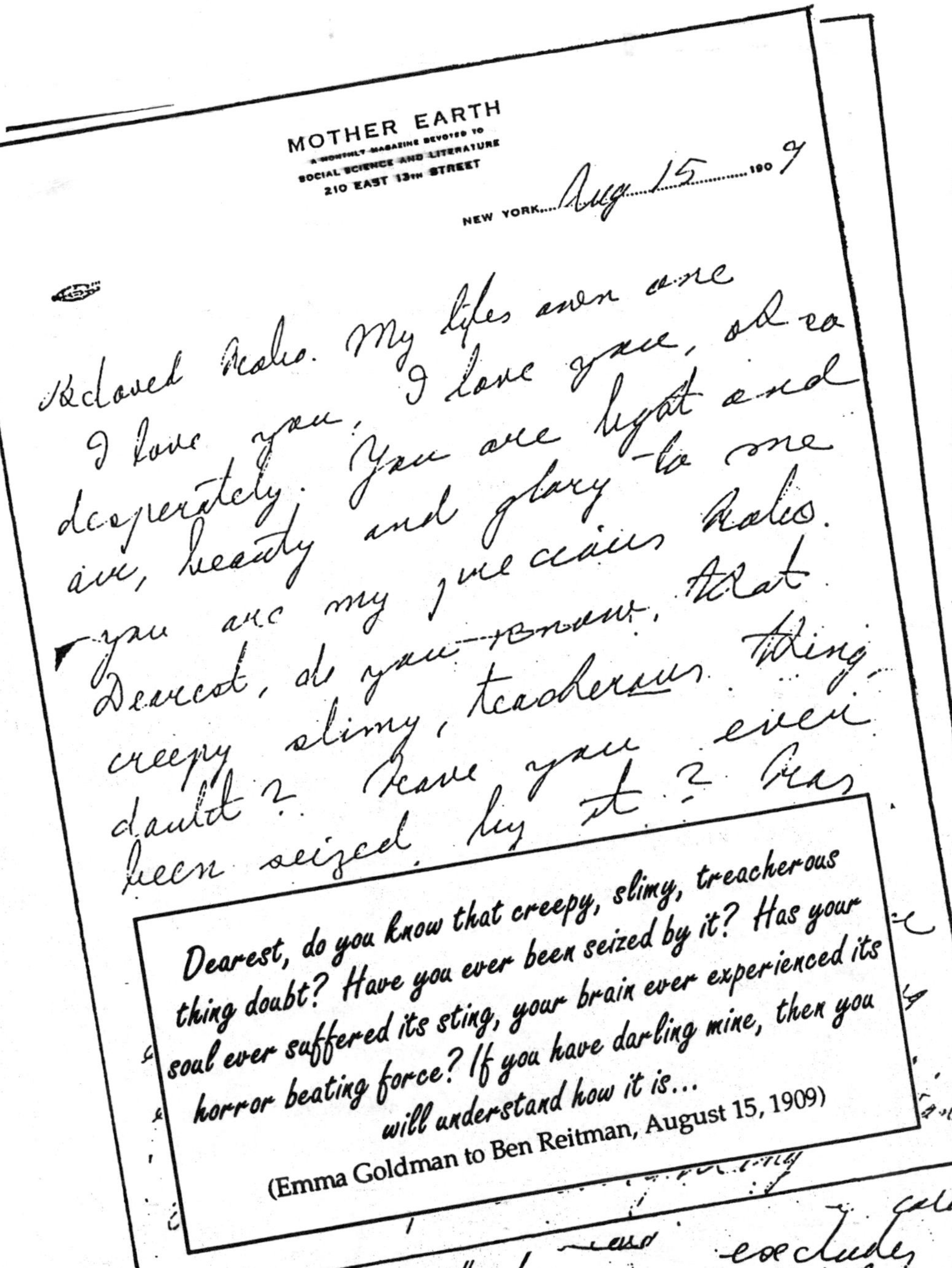

MOTHER EARTH
A MONTHLY MAGAZINE DEVOTED TO SOCIAL SCIENCE AND LITERATURE
210 EAST 13th STREET
NEW YORK Aug 15 1909

Beloved Hobo. My life's own one
I love you. I love you, oh so
desperately. You are light and
air, beauty and glory to me
you are my precious Hobo.
Dearest, do you know that
creepy slimy, treacherous thing,
doubt? Have you ever
been seized by it? Has

Dearest, do you know that creepy, slimy, treacherous thing doubt? Have you ever been seized by it? Has your soul ever suffered its sting, your brain ever experienced its horror beating force? If you have darling mine, then you will understand how it is...

(Emma Goldman to Ben Reitman, August 15, 1909)

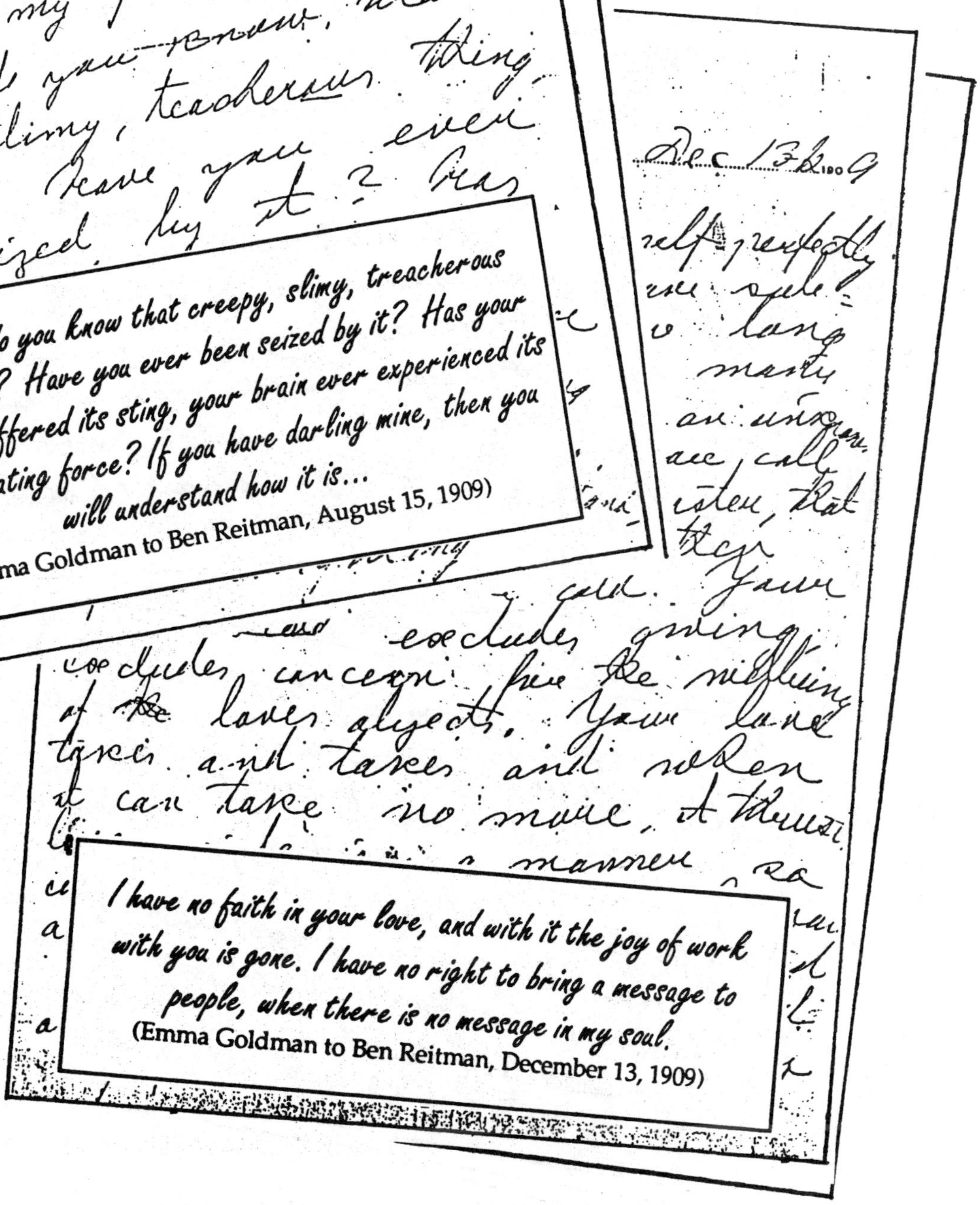

Dec 13th 1909

I have no faith in your love, and with it the joy of work with you is gone. I have no right to bring a message to people, when there is no message in my soul.

(Emma Goldman to Ben Reitman, December 13, 1909)

Ben L. Reitman, c. 1912

Original letters housed at the University of Illinois at Chicago Library.

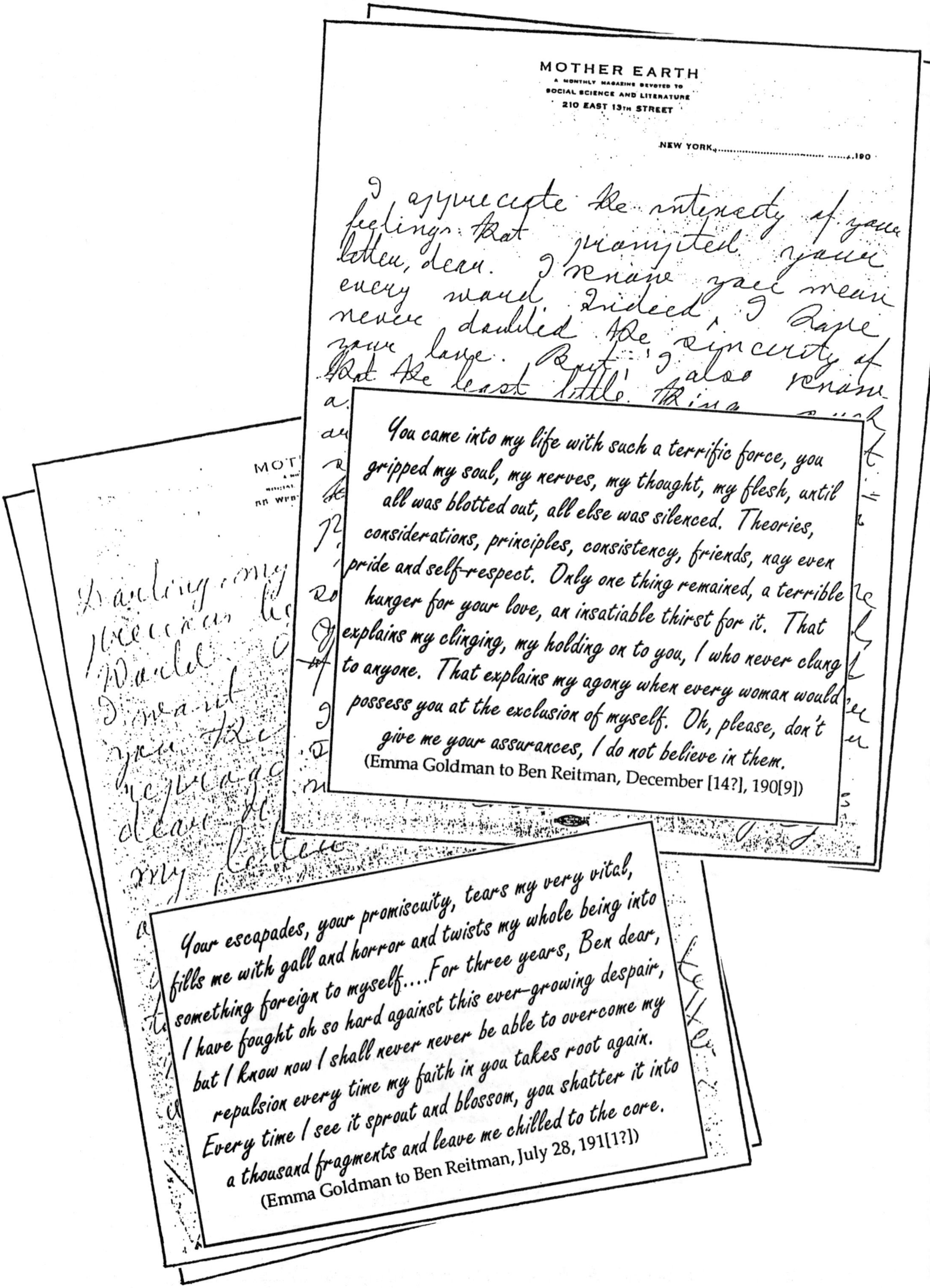

MOTHER EARTH
A MONTHLY MAGAZINE DEVOTED TO
SOCIAL SCIENCE AND LITERATURE
210 EAST 13TH STREET

NEW YORK, ... 190

You came into my life with such a terrific force, you gripped my soul, my nerves, my thought, my flesh, until all was blotted out, all else was silenced. Theories, considerations, principles, consistency, friends, nay even pride and self-respect. Only one thing remained, a terrible hunger for your love, an insatiable thirst for it. That explains my clinging, my holding on to you, I who never clung to anyone. That explains my agony when every woman would possess you at the exclusion of myself. Oh, please, don't give me your assurances, I do not believe in them.

(Emma Goldman to Ben Reitman, December [14?], 190[9])

Your escapades, your promiscuity, tears my very vital, fills me with gall and horror and twists my whole being into something foreign to myself....For three years, Ben dear, I have fought oh so hard against this ever-growing despair, but I know now I shall never never be able to overcome my repulsion every time my faith in you takes root again. Every time I see it sprout and blossom, you shatter it into a thousand fragments and leave me chilled to the core.

(Emma Goldman to Ben Reitman, July 28, 191[1?])

Original letters housed at the University of Illinois at Chicago Library.

Document Sixteen

Goldman Letter to the Press on "birth control and the necessity of imparting knowledge on this most vital question" (1916)

(from the International Institute of Social History, Amsterdam)

Context: An early advocate of birth control, Goldman addressed large audiences on the subject. Because dissemination of birth control information was forbidden by the Comstock Law, anyone who chose to speak out on the subject risked arrest, imprisonment, and fines. A few days after her arrest in New York City on February 11, 1916, Goldman wrote a letter to the press stating her position.

Questions on the document:

Describe what happened to Emma Goldman when she gave a lecture on birth control.
Why was her lecture considered illegal?
What did Emma Goldman mean when she referred to Anthony Comstock?
Why do you think Goldman began her letter by trying to separate her reputation as an anarchist from her activities on behalf of the birth control movement?
What do you think of Goldman's idea that people have a right to break or get rid of a law when it has outgrown time and necessity?

General Questions:

Is it illegal today to speak publicly on the topic of birth control? Abortion?
Is it illegal today to have an abortion? What are the moral and political arguments for and against abortion rights?
If you were in favor of affecting abortion laws, what tactics would you use to sway public opinion?
Do you think that planned parenthood organizations should be required to inform parents when a minor seeks birth control devices?
Do you think that the government should play a role in legislating women's reproductive functions? Why or why not?

MOTHER EARTH
Monthly Magazine
of
Anarchist Thought
10c. a Copy
$1.00 per Year

HEADQUARTERS FOR ANARCHIST LITERATURE

TEL. 6194 HARLEM

MOTHER EARTH PUBLISHING ASSOCIATION
20 EAST 125TH STREET
NEW YORK

ANARCHISM
The philosophy of a new social order based on liberty unrestricted by man-made law; the theory that all forms of government rest on violence, and are therefore wrong and harmful, as well as unnecessary

My dear Sir:-

In view of the fact that the Birth Control question is now dominant before the American public, I hope that you will not permit your prejudice against anarchism and myself as its exponent to refuse me fair play. I have lived and worked in New York City for twenty-five years. On more than one occasion I have been misrepresented in the press and anarchism has been made to appear hideous and ridiculous. I am not complaining; I am merely stating a fact which you, I am sure, know as well as I.

But now the question involved in my arrest which took place Friday, February 11th and which is to be heard Monday, February 28th is birth control, a world wide movement sponsored and supported by the greatest men and women through Europe and America, such as Prof. August Forel, Havelock Ellis, George Bernard Shaw, H. G. Wells, Dr. Drysdale in Europe and in America by Prof. Jacobi, Dr. Robinson and many others. A movement which has originated in minds of people who were both scientific and humanitarian, and which at the present time is backed by science, sociology and economic necessity. Certainly you will not refuse me a hearing in behalf of such an issue.

I have lectured on birth control for years; many times in New York and other cities, before representative audiences. At almost every meeting plain clothes men were present taking copious notes. It was therefore no secret that I am sponsoring birth control and the necessity of imparting knowledge on this most vital question.

Friday, February 4th, I again delivered this lecture in Forward Hall, New York, when three thousand people attempted to crowd the place. As a result of this popular clamor for knowledge on birth control, another meeting was arranged for Tuesday, February 8th at the New Star Casino. Again an eager throng attended. The meeting was orderly and everything went off as peacefully and intelligently as on all other occasions when I lecture if not interfered with by the police. Then on Friday, February 11th, just as I was about to enter the Forward Hall to deliver a lecture on Atheism, a subject which has no bearing at all upon birth control, I was arrested, taken to a filthy station house, then hustled into a patrol wagon, rushed to the Clinton Street jail, there searched in the most vulgar manner by a course looking matron in the presence of two detectives, a thing which would outrage the most hardened criminal. Then I was locked up in a cell until my bondsman released me on five hundred dollars bail.

Now all this was unnecessary in as much as I am too well known in the country to run away. Besides, one who has stood the brunt for an ideal for twenty-five years is not likely to run away. A summons would have been enough. But because I happen to be Emma Goldman and the exponent of Anarchism, the whole brutality of the

MOTHER EARTH
Monthly Magazine
of
Anarchist Thought
10c. a Copy
$1.00 per Year

HEADQUARTERS FOR ANARCHIST LITERATURE

TEL. 6194 HARLEM

MOTHER EARTH PUBLISHING ASSOCIATION
20 EAST 125TH STREET
NEW YORK

ANARCHISM
The philosophy of a new social order based on liberty unrestricted by man-made law; the theory that all forms of government rest on violence, and are therefore wrong and harmful, as well as unnecessary

New York police had to be employed in dealing with me, which only goes to prove that everything else in society advances except the Police Department. I confess I was credulous enough to believe that some change had taken place since my last arrest in New York City, which was in 1906, but I discovered my mistake.

However, this is not vital, but what is of importance and that which I hope you will place before your leaders is the fact that the methods of persecution of the part of the reactionary element in New York City in relation to any modern idea pertaining to birth control have evidently not ended with the death of Anthony Comstock. His successor, wanting to ingratiate himself, is leaving nothing undone to make any intelligent discussion of that vital subject possible. Unfortunately, he and the police are evidently not aware that birth control has reached such dimensions that no amount of persecution and petty chicanery can halt its sweep.

It is hardly necessary to point out that whatever may be the law on birth control, those like myself who are disseminating knowledge along that line are not doing so because of personal gain or because we consider it lewd or obscene. We do it because we know the desparate condition among the masses of workers and even professional people, when they cannot meet the demands of numerous children. It is upon that ground that I mean to make my fight when I go into court. Unless I am very much mistaken, I am sustained in my contention by the fundamental principles in America, namely, that when a law has outgrown time and necessity, it must go and the only way to get rid of the law. is to awaken the public to the fact that it has outlived its purposes and that is precisely what I have been doing and mean to do in the future.

I am planning a campaign of publicity through a large meeting in Carnegie Hall and through every other channel that will reach the intelligent American public to the fact that while I am not particularly anxious to go to jail, I should yet be glad to do so, if thereby I can add my might to the importance of birth control and the wiping off our antiquated law upon the statute.

Hoping that you will not refuse to acquaint your readers with the facts set forth here.

Sincerely yours,

Document Seventeen

Photograph of Goldman speaking on birth control, Union Square, New York City, May 20, 1916

Context: Emma Goldman and other birth control advocates distributed twenty thousand circulars on the day this photograph was taken. Although Goldman had been arrested previously for distributing birth control information, she continued to agitate on the issue, organizing mass meetings in halls and, as this photograph shows, in the open air.

Questions on the document:
Read the photograph:
What is going on?
What is the speaker using for a platform?
Where is the gathering?
Who are the people listening to her?
Where are the women?
What does this photograph say about Goldman's personality?
Can the photograph tell you anything about the attitude of the crowd?
Does this appear to be a legal gathering?

General Questions:
How is your conception of an historical figure or event affected when you see a photograph of that person or event? Can you name examples of photographs that have influenced your view of history?

Goldman Speaking on Birth Control, Union Square, New York City, 1916.

[illegible] at the International Institute of Social History, Amsterdam)

Document Eighteen

a. Excerpt from "Woman Suffrage" in *Anarchism and Other Essays* by Emma Goldman (1910)

b. *New York Times* headline, "Suffrage Army Out on Parade" (1912)

Context: Female suffrage was a major reform goal of the Progressive Era. Emma Goldman, however, did not believe that the ballot would secure equality for women. She rejected the idea, which many suffragists held, that by voting women would clean up politics.

Questions on the document:
Is Goldman opposed to women gaining the right to vote?
What does she say about the idea that women will "purify" politics and government?
Why does she describe the suffrage movement as a "parlor affair"?
Does Goldman see equality within the suffrage movement? Explain.
If you were a suffragist, how would you answer Goldman's criticism?

General Questions:
In your school, are there an equal number of males and females in elected offices? What positions do the females hold? the males?
If a candidate in your school ran a campaign focused on women's issues, what would those issues be?
Would a candidate's gender influence your decision to support him or her?
Is there such a thing as a "woman's vote"? How would you define it?
How would more women in public office make a difference?

Excerpt from "Woman Suffrage" by Emma Goldman (1910)
Published in *Anarchism and Other Essays.*

The poor, stupid, free American citizen! Free to starve, free to tramp the highways of this great country, he enjoys universal suffrage, and, by that right, he has forged chains about his limbs. The reward that he receives is stringent labor laws prohibiting the right of boycott, of picketing, in fact, of everything, except the right to be robbed of the fruits of his labor. Yet all these disastrous results of the twentieth-century fetich have taught woman nothing. But, then, woman will purify politics, we are assured.

Needless to say, I am not opposed to woman suffrage on the conventional ground that she is not equal to it. I see neither physical, psychological, nor mental reasons why woman should not have the equal right to vote with man. But that can not possibly blind me to the absurd notion that woman will accomplish that wherein man has failed. If she would not make things worse, she certainly could not make them better. To assume, therefore, that she would succeed in purifying something which is not susceptible of purification, is to credit her with supernatural powers. Since woman's greatest misfortune has been that she was looked upon as either angel or devil, her true salvation lies in being placed on earth; namely, in being considered human, and therefore subject to all human follies and mistakes. Are we, then, to believe that two errors will make a right? Are we to assume that the poison already inherent in politics will be decreased, if women were to enter the political arena? The most ardent suffragists would hardly maintain such a folly. . . .

The American suffrage movement has been, until very recently, altogether a parlor affair, absolutely detached from the economic needs of the people. Thus Susan B. Anthony, no doubt an exceptional type of woman, was not only indifferent but antagonistic to labor; nor did she hesitate to manifest her antagonism when, in 1869, she advised women to take the places of striking printers in New York.† I do not know whether her attitude had changed before her death.

There are, of course, some suffragists who are affiliated with workingwomen—the Women's Trade Union League, for instance; but they are a small minority, and their activities are essentially economic. The rest look upon toil as a just provision of Providence. What would become of the rich, if not for the poor? What would become of these idle, parasitic ladies, who squander more in a week than their victims earn in a year, if not for the eighty million wage-workers? Equality, who ever heard of such a thing?

SUFFRAGE ARMY OUT ON PARADE

Perhaps 10,000 Women and Men Sympathizers March for the Cause.

STREETS PACKED FOR THEM

Cheers for the Women and Some Good-Natured Jesting at the Men.

AGED LEADERS APPLAUDED

They Rode in Flower-Bedecked Carriages—Women on Horseback and "Joan of Arc" Win Plaudits.

New York Times, May 5, 1912

† *Equal Suffrage*, Dr. Helen A. Sumner.

Topic Three: Women's Rights
Suggested Activities

Assign roles and act out the interview from the *St. Louis Post-Dispatch* (Document Fourteen).

Pretend you are Emma Goldman on a talk show. Comment on the institution of marriage today.

Write a letter to Goldman about the changes that have occurred in the institution of marriage since her time.

Research the Comstock Law. Find out how it was used to stop the dissemination of birth control information.

Identify contemporary pro-choice and anti-abortion organizations. Gather news articles summarizing their arguments for and against a woman's right to control her reproductive life. Hold a debate.

Research laws regulating a man's reproductive rights.

Find out what medical, sociological, and economic arguments in favor of birth control were used in 1916. Compare and contrast arguments for and against birth control presented in the early years of the century with today's arguments on abortion.

Use the documents on Goldman to compare and contrast her ideas and actions with another prominent woman of the Progressive Era: for example, labor leader Elizabeth Gurley Flynn, social worker Jane Addams, African-American journalist Ida B. Wells Barnett, Jewish labor organizer Rose Schneiderman.

Find out more about the ideas of birth control pioneers, including Havelock Ellis, Olive Schreiner, Dr. Dorothy Bocker, Dr. Hannah Stone, Helen Keller, Margaret Sanger.

Students role play one of the above-listed personalities of their choice. Hold a forum in the class in which audience members ask questions of each personality addressing such issues as love, marriage, female equality, sexuality, suffrage.

TOPIC FOUR
Anti-Militarism

TOPIC FOUR: Anti-Militarism

These documents highlight the nationwide debates that preceded U.S. entry into World War I. They examine:

- Preparedness—the buildup of American armed forces, thought by some to be insurance against war, but in fact the prelude to intervention in the European war.

- Conscription—the involuntary induction into military service which antiwar activists campaigned against.

- Militarism—military buildup in times of war and peace and the corresponding glorification of a military spirit.

Background to the documents: Emma Goldman opposed involuntary military service in part because of her childhood experiences in Czarist Russia where state officials periodically seized young men off the streets to serve in the army, and also because she was an anarchist who believed in free choice in all aspects of life. By 1917, she was vigorously involved in fighting America's march toward war. Goldman believed Woodrow Wilson's campaign to prepare the United States for war would result in a militarized America. Goldman even attacked Wilson's position of neutrality, stating: "It is not enough to claim being neutral; a neutrality which sheds crocodile tears with one eye and keeps the other riveted upon the profits from war supplies and war loans is not neutrality." She protested the involuntary drafting of young men into the military. Her anti-conscription activities led to her arrest, imprisonment, and, ultimately, her deportation. The following documents illustrate Goldman's opposition to conscription, her concerns about military buildup, and the organized efforts to oppose conscription.

Document Nineteen

**a. Excerpt from Goldman's lecture/pamphlet:
"Preparedness: The Road to Universal Slaughter" (1915)**

b. World War I propaganda poster

c. Political cartoon by Robert Minor (1917)

Context: President Woodrow Wilson initiated a program of military preparedness despite his intent to keep the United States out of World War I. He held that preparedness, the building up of America's military might, was the best insurance against America's entry into the conflict. Goldman, on the other hand, saw preparedness as the inevitable road to war.

Questions on the document:
Why was war the inevitable result of military preparedness according to Emma Goldman?
What graphic images does she use to describe preparedness?
Why does Goldman call America a melting pot? Does the concept of American nationalism conflict with this idea?
What were the economic and social effects of military preparedness?
Based on her observations in Europe at that time, how does Goldman frame her fears for America's future?
From Goldman's perspective, how do German and American militarism differ?
Why does Goldman criticize President Woodrow Wilson more than former president Theodore Roosevelt?
What did the phrase, "America for the Americans" mean, and which of the groups mentioned in Goldman's essay rallied in support of this slogan?

General Questions:
Does a nation's military strength promote or prevent it from going to war?
Is it unpatriotic to actively resist U.S. involvement in a war? What factors influence your judgment?
What groups gain and what groups lose from militarism?
Can you give examples of times and places when military buildup has led to war? When it has prevented war?
In times of war, can a democratic government justify limiting First Amendment rights of free speech in the name of national security?

Excerpt from "Preparedness: The Road to Universal Slaughter"

by Emma Goldman (1915)

Ammunition! Ammunition! O, Lord, thou who rulest heaven and earth, thou God of love, of mercy and of justice, provide us with enough ammunition to destroy our enemy. Such is the prayer which is ascending daily to the Christian heaven. Just like cattle, panic-stricken in the face of fire, throw themselves into the very flames, so all of the European people have fallen over each other into the devouring flames of the furies of war, and America, pushed to the very brink by unscrupulous politicians, by ranting demagogues, and by military sharks, is preparing for the same terrible feat...

Wartime propaganda poster
(State Historical Society of Wisconsin, Madison)

America is essentially the melting pot. No national unit composing it is in a position to boast of superior race purity, particular historic mission, or higher culture. Yet the jingoes and war speculators are filling the air with the sentimental slogan of hypocritical nationalism, "America for Americans," "America first, last, and all the time." This cry has caught the popular fancy from one end of the country to another. In order to maintain America, military preparedness must be engaged in at once. A billion dollars of the people's sweat and blood is to be expended for dreadnaughts and submarines for the army and the navy, all to protect this precious America.

The pathos of it all is that the America which is to be protected by a huge military force is not the America of the people, but that of the privileged class; the class which robs and exploits the masses, and controls their lives from the cradle to the grave. No less pathetic is it that so few people realize that preparedness never leads to peace, but that it is indeed the road to universal slaughter...

Since the war began, miles of paper and oceans of ink have been used to prove the barbarity, the cruelty, the oppression of Prussian militarism. Conservatives and radicals alike are giving their support to the Allies for no other reason than to help crush that militarism, in the presence of which, they say, there can be no peace or progress in Europe. But though America grows fat on the manufacture of munitions and war loans to the Allies to help crush Prussians the same cry is now being raised in America which, if carried into national action, would build up an American militarism far more terrible than German or Prussian militarism could ever be, and that because nowhere in the world has capitalism become so brazen in its greed and nowhere is the state so ready to kneel at the feet of capital.

Like a plague, the mad spirit is sweeping the country, infesting the clearest heads and staunchest hearts with the deathly germ of militarism. National security leagues, with cannon as their emblem of protection, naval leagues with women in their lead have sprung up all over the country, women who boast of representing the gentler sex, women who in pain and danger bring forth life and yet are ready to dedicate it to the Moloch War. Americanization societies with well known liberals as members, they who but yesterday decried the patriotic clap-trap of to-day, are now lending themselves to befog the minds of the people and to help build up the same destructive institutions in America which they are directly and indirectly helping to pull down in Germany—militarism, the destroyer of youth, the raper of women, the annihilator of the best in the race, the very mower of life.

'At last I have found the ideal soldier who will keep quiet and carry out orders without arguing.'
Cartoon by Robert Minor from Golos Truda
(Petrograd, October 27, 1917)

Even Woodrow Wilson, who not so long ago indulged in the phrase, "A nation too proud to fight," who in the beginning of the war ordered prayers for peace, who in his proclamations spoke of the necessity of watchful waiting, even he has been whipped into line. He has now joined his worthy colleagues in the jingo movement, echoing their clamor for preparedness and their howl of "America for Americans." The difference between Wilson and Roosevelt is this: Roosevelt , a born bully, uses the club; Wilson, the historian, the college professor, wears the smooth polished university mask, but underneath it he, like Roosevelt, has but one aim, to serve the big interests, to add to those who are growing phenomenally rich by the manufacture of military supplies...

That which has driven the masses of Europe into the trenches and to the battlefields is not their inner longing for war; it must be traced to the cut-throat competition for military equipment, for more efficient armies, for larger warships, for more powerful cannon. You cannot build up a standing army and then throw it back into a box like tin soldiers. Armies equipped to the teeth with weapons, with highly developed instruments of murder and backed by their military interests, have their own dynamic functions. We have but to examine into the nature of militarism to realize the truism of this contention.

Militarism consumes the strongest and most productive elements of each nation. Militarism swallows the largest part of the national revenue. Almost nothing is spent on education, art, literature and science compared with the amount devoted to militarism in times of peace, while in times of war everything else is set at naught; all life stagnates, all effort is curtailed; the very sweat and blood of the masses are used to feed this insatiable monster—militarism. Under such circumstances, it must become more arrogant, more aggressive, more bloated with its own importance. If for no other reason, it is out of surplus energy that militarism must act to remain alive; therefore it will seek an enemy or create one artificially. In this civilized purpose and method, militarism is sustained by the state, protected by the laws of the land, fostered by the home and the school, and glorified by public opinion. In other words, the function of militarism is to kill. It cannot live except through murder.

Document Twenty

Mother Earth Cover by Man Ray, 1914

Context: Man Ray (Emmanuel Radnitsky) was a modern school artist. Like Emma Goldman, he took an antiwar position. His antiwar cartoons appeared in her *Mother Earth* magazine.

Questions on the document:

Examine this cover: What military conflict is being depicted? Do you see a flag? What people are shown? What do you think the artist meant by: the crucifix symbol, the prisoners, the bars? How do you interpret this cartoon?

How does this drawing serve to illustrate arguments made by Goldman in the pamphlet, "Preparedness: The Road to Universal Slaughter"?

MOTHER EARTH

Vol. IX. September, 1914 No. 7

PRICE 10 CENTS

Document Twenty-One

No-Conscription League Manifesto, 1917

(from Records of the Department of War and Military Intelligence Division, Record Group 165, National Archives)

Context: Once the United States entered World War I in April 1917, President Wilson signed a Draft Bill setting June 4th as Registration Day for men aged twenty-one to thirty-one. Emma Goldman and her colleague Alexander Berkman helped organize the No-Conscription League which held a series of antiwar rallies to discourage young men from registering for the draft. There follows a copy of the manifesto that the group circulated to over 100,000 people. On June 15, 1917, Goldman and Berkman were arrested and charged with conspiracy to obstruct the draft. After they were found guilty, the judge sentenced them to two years in prison and recommended their deportation once they had served their sentence.

Questions on the document:
What is the man in this illustration doing? What statement is he making through his actions? According to the manifesto: what is a conscientious objector? How does the conscription of citizens into the military threaten individual liberty? What group gains and what group loses from conscription?

General Questions:
In addition to the points made in the No-Conscription League platform, what other reasons might justify refusing to serve in the military?
In which other American wars were men conscripted to fight? Has the United States been the only country to have conscientious objectors?
Today, what is the government position toward conscientious objectors?
Research newspapers and magazines to learn about the experience of conscientious objectors during the Gulf War or the Vietnam War. Does the strength of public support or opposition to wars influence the decision-making process of conscientious objectors and their subsequent treatment?

NO CONSCRIPTION!

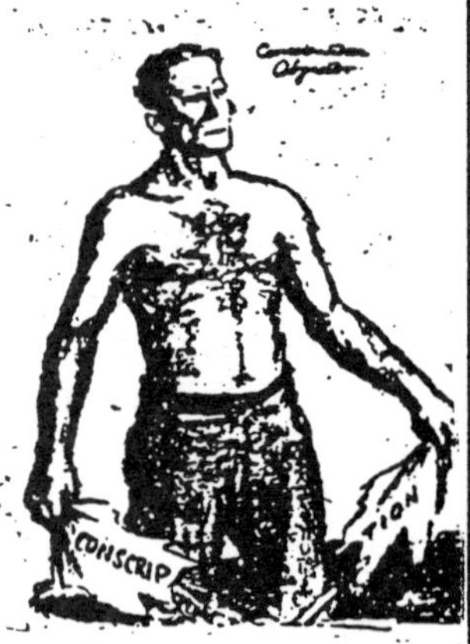

CONSCRIPTION has now become a fact in this country. It took England fully 18 months after she engaged in the war to impose compulsory military service on her people. It was left for "free" America to pass a conscription bill six weeks after she declared war against Germany.

What becomes of the patriotic boast of America to have entered the European war in behalf of the principle of democracy? But that is not all. Every country in Europe has recognized the right of conscientious objectors—of men who refuse to engage in war on the ground that they are opposed to taking life. Yet this democratic country makes no such provision for those who will not commit murder at the behest of the war profiteers. Thus the "land of the free and the home of the brave" is ready to coerce free men into the military yoke.

No one to whom the fundamental principle of liberty and justice is more than an idle phrase, can help realize that the patriotic clap-trap now shouted by press, pulpit and the authorities, betrays a desperate effort of the ruling class in this country to throw sand in the eyes of the masses and to blind them to the real issue confronting them. That issue is the Prussianizing of America so as to destroy whatever few liberties the people have achieved through an incessant struggle of many years.

Already all labor protective laws have been abrogated, which means that while husbands, fathers and sons are butchered on the battlefield, the women and children will be exploited in our industrial bastiles to the heart's content of the American patriots for gain and power.

Freedom of speech, of press and assembly is about to be thrown upon the dungheap of political guarantees. But crime of all crimes, the flower of the country is to be forced into murder whether or not they believe in war or in the efficacy of saving democracy in Europe by the destruction of democracy at home.

Liberty of conscience is the most fundamental of all human rights, the pivot of all progress. No man may be deprived of it without losing every vestige of freedom of thought and action. In these days when every principle and conception of democracy and individual liberty is being cast overboard under the pretext of democratizing Germany, it behooves every liberty-loving man and woman to insist on his or her right of individual choice in the ordering of his life and actions.

The NO-CONSCRIPTION LEAGUE has been formed for the purpose of encouraging conscientious objectors to affirm their liberty of conscience and to make their objection to human slaughter effective by refusing to participate in the killing of their fellow men. The NO-CONSCRIPTION LEAGUE is to be the voice of protest against the coercion of conscientious objectors to participate in the war. Our platform may be summarized as follows:

> We oppose conscription because we are internationalists, anti-militarists, and opposed to all wars waged by capitalistic governments.
>
> We will fight for what we choose to fight for; we will never fight simply because we are ordered to fight.
>
> We believe that the militarization of America is an evil that far outweighs, in its anti-social and anti-libertarian effects, any good that may come from America's participation in the war.
>
> We will resist conscription by every means in our power, and we will sustain those who, for similar reasons, refuse to be conscripted.

We are not unmindful of the difficulties in our way. But we have resolved to go ahead and spare no effort to make the voice of protest a moral force in the life of this country. The initial efforts of the conscientious objectors in England were fraught with many hardships and danger, but finally the government of Great Britain was forced to give heed to the steadily increasing volume of public protest against the coercion of conscientious objectors. So we, too, in America, will doubtless meet the full severity of the government and the condemnation of the war-mad jingoes, but we are nevertheless determined to go ahead. We feel confident in arousing thousands of people who are conscientious objectors to the murder of their fellowmen and to whom a principle represents the most vital thing in life.

Resist conscription. Organize meetings. Join our League. Send us money. Help us to give assistance to those who come in conflict with the government. Help us to publish literature against militarism and against conscription.

We consider this campaign of the utmost importance at the present time. Amid hateful, cowardly silence, a powerful voice and an all-embracing love are necessary to make the living dead shiver.

NO-CONSCRIPTION LEAGUE
20 East 125th St., New York.

Topic Four: Anti-Militarism
Suggested Activities

Collect newspaper or magazine reports on current wars. Address these questions: What arguments for fighting do the combatants offer? Are other nations or groups within the country at war working to stop this war? What ideas can you offer to bring an end to this conflict?

Write for information from organizations such as the *Veterans of Foreign Wars, US Marine Corps, Wheelchair Veterans of America, Women's International League for Peace and Freedom, Women for Peace, American Friends Service Committee's youth militarism project, Pledge of Resistance, Vietnam Veterans against the War.* Compare information you receive, and use it to create posters presenting the different points of view.

Using one of Woodrow Wilson's public speeches on preparedness and Goldman's preparedness pamphlet, hold a mock rally in which speakers give speeches representing the views of both.

Gather statements from conscientious objectors in any of America's wars. Describe the circumstances and consequence of the statements.

Collect contemporary pro- and antimilitary cartoons from newspapers and magazines. Make your own cartoons illustrating your view.

Look into the origins of the philosophical concept of a "just war." What American conflicts do you think exemplify this concept?

Research the experiences of African-American people during the World War I period. What led to the Silent March on Fifth Avenue in New York City on July 28, 1917? Did racism affect African-American people's attitudes toward the war? How have other domestic issues affected public views of foreign policies?

Using the sources listed in the bibliography, research a variety of views about war espoused by contemporaries of Goldman such as Eugene Debs, Jane Addams, Theodore Roosevelt, Woodrow Wilson, and Randolph Bourne. Which wars were the following individuals most closely associated with and what stance did they take on those wars: General Douglas MacArthur, Richard Nixon, Jean Kirkpatrick, Henry Kissinger, Martin Luther King, Jr., and Daniel Ellsberg. Compare their positions with those of Goldman's contemporaries.

TOPIC FIVE

Art and Literature of Social Change

TOPIC FIVE: Art and Literature of Social Change

Emma Goldman recognized the power of art and literature to influence and inspire political awareness and action. Her love of the modern drama and her interest in classic literary works as well as the new artists and photographers of her time was evident in her lectures and in her magazine, *Mother Earth.* She believed that exposure to the beauty of literature and art should not be the exclusive privilege of the rich and educated, but should be an integral part of everyday life for all people. Goldman was as comfortable giving a lecture on the social significance of modern drama to an exclusive women's literary club one day, as she was giving the same lecture to coal miners in a mineshaft the next day. What she drew from most of these theatrical performances and artistic expressions was the dignity and beauty of small individual acts of courage in daily life that make the vision of social harmony a tangible possibility. The documents included here discuss:

- Drama—its potential as a mirror of the society.
- Poetry—as source of inspiration.
- Art—as it experiments with forms and representations of social issues, and its accompanying bohemian subculture.

Background to the documents: In turn-of-the century New York and western Europe, artists and social activists alike challenged conventional forms and ideas. The excitement of the discovery of new ways of looking at the world and envisioning the future created a lively international bohemian culture, of which Emma Goldman was a part.

Document Twenty-Two

a. *New York Times* report on the Armory Show, "Cubists and Futurists Are Making Insanity Pay," March 16, 1913
b. Robert Minor illustration on *Mother Earth* cover, October 1915

Context: Goldman's challenging political ideas were in complete accord with the simultaneous revolution taking place in the art world. The 1913 Armory Show in New York introduced European modernist painters like Matisse, Picasso, Van Gogh, and Gauguin. Such a departure from conventional representational art was considered by some a threat to wholesome American values. Post-impressionism was interpreted as "the harbinger of universal anarchy...denial of all law,...insurrection against all custom and tradition,...assertion of individual licence without discipline and without restraint." The immediate link between politics and art was heralded as a victory of internationalism by some, and as a sign of the disintegration of culture and custom by others. The new art did in fact supplant the old, and its force could not be censored. Many artists associated with the bohemian culture of Greenwich Village and the "Ash Can School" (which included Goldman's associate Robert Henri) were also closely linked to political radicalism.

The early 1900s was also a fertile time for artists in the United States to create a new kind of political satire. With the blossoming of "little magazines" like *The Masses*, *Mother Earth*, and *The Little Review*, artists like Robert Minor, George Bellows, Man Ray, and Boardman Robinson added a powerful visual dimension to these political and literary publications. Many of these artists also taught at the Ferrer Modern School, founded by Goldman and other New York anarchists.

Questions on the documents:
What perspective is revealed in the *New York Times* article on the Armory Show?
What is it that Kenyon Cox feared?
Does this recounting of the 1913 art show resonate with anything in your current experience with respect to art or music?

What does Robert Minor's illustration imply about the source of labor's strength within the courts?
What was happening in the country at this time for workers?
How does this visual image enhance the message of the labor movement?

General Questions:
Why is anarchism so often linked to the fear of chaos, in politics and in art?
In what way do the visual arts reflect cultural values and trends?
Can government censorship of art or ideas ever be a positive social value?
Should there be a uniform language of art?
How is freedom of expression in art related to your own freedom?

Can you find examples of political satire in the imagery in comics, television, advertising, or films?
Can you create your own visual social commentary?

Magazine Section
Part Six

The New York Times.

SUNDAY, MARCH 16, 1913.

Magazine Section
Part Six

"CUBISTS AND FUTURISTS ARE MAKING INSANITY PAY"

[Ke]nyon Cox, Member of the National Academy, and Recognized Here and Abroad as One of America's Foremost Painters, Gives a Straight-from-the-Shoulder Opinion of the New Movements in Art.

ANOTHER OF THE RODIN DRAWINGS

"UNE MUSE"
A PROGRESSIVE BUST

THE MUCH DISCUSSED "NUDE DESCENDING A STAIRCASE"

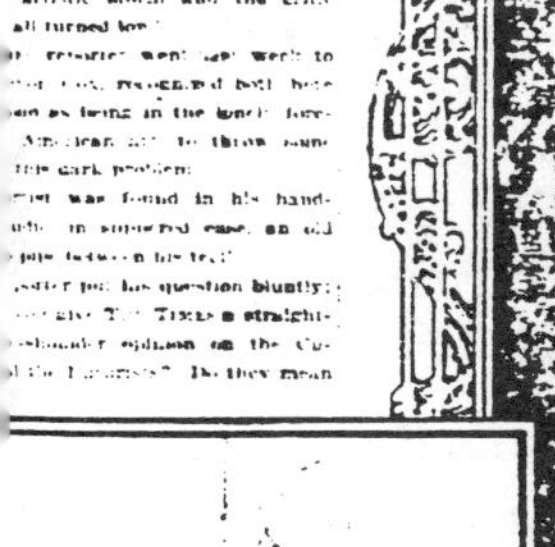

A RODIN DRAWING AT THE METROPOLITAN

Excerpts from newspaper article begin on next page.

What does the work of the Cubists and Futurists mean? Have these "progressives" really outstripped all the rest of us, glimpsed the future, and used a form of artistic expression that is simply esoteric to the great laggard public? Is their work a conspicuous milestone in the progress of art? Or is it junk?

The International Exhibition of Modern Art, which has just come to a close in the Sixty-ninth Regiment Armory, with its striking array of the works of the "progressives," has during the past few weeks, set many a New Yorker to turning this problem over in his mind.

Entirely apart from the canvases and sculptures shown, this exhibition was unique among New York exhibitions. It drew an attendance from a public outside that comparatively limited one that ordinarily goes to art exhibitions.

Here was something revolutionary, something in the nature of a nine-days' wonder, something that must not be missed. New York did not miss it: the gate receipts show that.

How the Public Acted.

A good part of New York grinned as it passed along from one paint-puzzle to another. But the fact that there were so many of these paint-puzzles, that they were dignified by an exhibition, made New York, in spite of its grin, wonder if there perhaps was not something in this new art which was a little beyond the mental grasp of the uninitiated.

In circles where art had never before been discussed, one heard the question:

"Have you been to see the Cubists and the Futurists? Yes? Well, could you make anything out of it?"

The answer usually was:

"Why, I don't know much about art, but it looked to me like a mess of nonsense." ...

A TIMES reporter went last week to ask Kenyon Cox, recognized both here and abroad as being in the lonely forerank of American art, to throw some light on this dark problem.

The artist was found in his handsome studio, in slippered ease, an old corn-cob pipe between his teeth.

The reporter put his question bluntly:

"Will you give THE TIMES a straight-from-the-shoulder opinion on the Cubists and the Futurists? Do they mean something in art, or do they mean nothing?"

Mr. Cox took a reflective puff or two, gazed a moment at the few embers in the broad, stone fireplace as though marshalling his thoughts, and then came the straight-from-the-shoulder opinion.

"The Cubists and the Futurists simply abolish the art of painting. They deny not only any representation of nature, but also any known or traditional form of decoration.

"A New Language."

"They maintain that they have invented a symbolism which expresses their individuality, or as they say, their souls....

Talk to these people and they say:

"Here is a new language of art. You have no right to criticize until you learn it."

"My answer is:

"'What would you think of a poet or literary man suddenly inventing a new language and saying something that sounds like pure gibberish?' 'Ah,' he remarks in answer to your objections, 'you don't understand the language.'

A Strange Kind of Art.

"If this suppositious poet or literary man were to say 'Wigglety-wagglety-wigglety,' and then tell you that [any] combination of letters gives the [embod]iment of dawn, how are you going to prove that it doesn't?...

"Expression, no matter whether the medium be a painting, a sculpture, a novel, or a poem, must either be in a language that has been learned, or it is a pure assumption on the artists' part that he has expressed anything at all....

"There is one point, and one on which I feel strongly: This is not a sudden disruption or eruption in the history of art. It is the inevitable result of a tendency which has grown stronger and stronger during the last fifty years.

"It is a tendency to abandon all discipline, all respect for tradition, and to insist that art shall be nothing but an expression of the individual....

"The next step was for the Post-Impressionists to revolt again much discipline, to maintain that it does not matter how things look, the only point of importance being how you feel about them....

"They talk of their symbolism and their soul-expression!

"The thing is pathological! It's hideous!"

There was a pause. Then the old corncob was reached for; refilled; lighted.

"There is another element that comes into it," continued the artist when the corncob was comfortably under way. "Up to the time of Matisse, the revolutionaries, I believe, were for the most part sincere enough. They paid for their beliefs with their lives: they made no money out of their beliefs; they committed suicide or died in mad-houses.

"But with Matisse, with the later work of Rodin, and above all, with the Cubists and Futurists, it is no longer a matter of sincere fanaticism. These men have seized upon the modern engine of publicity and are making insanity pay.

Back to Matisse.

"I should perhaps interpolate here that a number of men who are responsible for the present movement have done some beautiful work, but that does not prevent me thinking that they are headed in the wrong direction.

"But, getting back to Matisse— If I wanted to mention names I could add others to the list—many of his paintings are simply the exaltation to the walls of a gallery of the drawings of a nasty boy.

"I have always championed the nude." (There are a number of large paintings of the nude on the walls of his studio.) "I am not squeamish on that side of the question: but I feel that in the drawings of some of these men there is a professed indecency which is absolutely shocking....

"What I have said to you is not the opinion of a conservative. It is founded on a lifetime given to the study of art and criticism, in the belief that painting means something....

"The great traditions of the world are not here by accident. They exist because humanity found them to be for its own good.

"Art has a social function. In all the great periods of art it has spoken to the people in a language that they understood and expressed what they would have it express.

"These men who would make art merely expressive of their personal whim, make it speak in a special language only understood by themselves, are as truly anarchists as are those who would overthrow all social laws.

"But the modern tendency is to exalt individualism at the expense of law. The Cubists and the Futurists simply exhibit a very extreme and savage form of this individualism...

Excerpted from New York Times *article, March 16, 1913*

MOTHER EARTH

Vol. X. October, 1915 No. 8

LABOR'S LAWYER

Document Twenty-Three

Excerpts from *The Social Significance of the Modern Drama* by Emma Goldman (1914): foreword, and essay on Henrik Ibsen's play, *A Doll's House*

Context: European drama at the turn of the century was a focal point for expressing social and political challenges to the status quo. Goldman lectured frequently on the social significance of modern drama, both because of her interest in the subject, and because in a time of extreme political repression, challenging ideas could sometimes only be expressed as "literary," not as "political" criticism.

Goldman was among the most prominent disseminators of European literary and artistic avant-garde ideas in the United States. She considered this aspect of her work integral to the overall anarchist vision of the liberation of the human spirit from the shackles of convention.

The excerpt from Goldman's essay on Ibsen's *A Doll's House* also illustrates the ways in which drama criticism can be a powerful vehicle for discussing the political aspect of the relationship between women and men.

Questions on the documents:
Is the artist's decision about what to paint or to write about an aesthetic and/or political decision? Why? Give an example from Goldman's texts, and then elaborate on your idea with a contemporary example.
Read the full text of *A Doll's House*, or watch the film, and comment on whether Goldman's interpretation of the play rings true.
How do you think that women's experiences in the home have changed, or are the issues of *A Doll's House* still contemporary?
What do you think happened to Nora after she left home?
Do you think the "gate of life for women" is different now than it was in Goldman's time?

General Questions:
Can you apply Goldman's analysis about the social significance of modern drama to the medium of film?
Can movies inspire people to change, and mirror life's struggles? Give an example.
Is it possible to write a play or a film script that is not subject to political analysis? Give examples.

FOREWORD

IN order to understand the social and dynamic significance of modern dramatic art it is necessary, I believe, to ascertain the difference between the functions of art for art's sake and art as the mirror of life.

Art for art's sake presupposes an attitude of aloofness on the part of the artist toward the complex struggle of life: he must rise about the ebb and tide of life. He is to be merely an artistic conjurer of beautiful forms, a creator of pure fancy.

That is not the attitude of modern art, which is preeminently the reflex, the mirror of life. The artist being a part of life cannot detach himself from the events and occurrences that pass panorama-like before his eyes, impressing themselves upon his emotional and intellectual vision.

The modern artist is, in the words of August Strindberg, "a lay preacher popularizing the pressing questions of his time." Not necessarily because his aim is to proselyte, but because he can best express himself by being true to life.

Millet, Meunier, Turgenev, Dostoyevsky, Emerson, Walt Whitman, Tolstoy, Ibsen, Strindberg, Hauptmann and a host of others mirror in their work as much of the spiritual and social revolt as is expressed by the most fiery speech of the propagandist. And more important still, they compel far greater attention. Their creative genius, imbued with the spirit of sincerity and truth, strikes root where the ordinary word often falls on barren soil.

The reason that many radicals as well as conservatives fail to grasp the powerful message of art is perhaps not far to seek. The average radical is as hidebound by mere terms as the man devoid of all ideas. "Bloated plutocrats," "economic determinism," "class consciousness," and similar expressions sum up for him the symbols of revolt. But since art speaks a language of its own, a language embracing the entire gamut of human emotions, it often sounds meaningless to those whose hearing has been dulled by the din of stereotyped phrases.

On the other hand, the conservative sees danger only in the advocacy of the Red Flag. He has too long been fed on the historic legend that it is only the "rabble" which makes revolutions, and not those who wield the brush or pen. It is therefore legitimate to applaud the artist and hound the rabble. Both radical and conservative have to learn that any mode of creative work, which with true perception portrays social wrongs earnestly and boldly, may be a greater menace to our social fabric and a more powerful inspiration than the wildest harangue of the soapbox orator.

Unfortunately, we in America have so far looked upon the theater as a place of amusement only, exclusive of ideas and inspiration. Because the modern drama of Europe has till recently been inaccessible in printed form to the average theater-goer in this country, he had to content himself with the interpretation, or rather misinterpretation, of our dramatic critics. As a result the social significance of the Modern Drama has well nigh been lost to the general public....

The Modern Drama, as all modern literature, mirrors the complex struggle of life,—the struggle which, whatever its individual or topical expression, ever has its roots in the depth of human nature and social environment, and hence is, to that extent, universal. Such literature, such drama, is at once the reflex and the inspiration of mankind in its eternal seeking for things higher and better. Perhaps those who learn the great truths of the social travail in the school of life, do not need the message of the drama. But there is another class whose number is legion, for whom that message is indispensable. ...another medium is needed to arouse the intellectuals of this country, to make them realize their relation to the people, to the social unrest permeating the atmosphere.

The medium which has the power to do that is the Modern Drama, because it mirrors every phase of life and embraces every strata of society,—...society has gone beyond the stage of patching up,...man must throw off the dead weight of the past, with all its ghosts and spooks, if he is to go foot free to meet the future.

This is the social significance which differentiates modern dramatic art from art for art's sake. It is the dynamite which undermines superstition, shakes the social pillars, and prepares men and women for the reconstruction.

Emma Goldman

Excerpted from *The Social Significance of The Modern Drama* by Emma Goldman (1914)

A DOLL'S HOUSE

IN "A Doll's House" Ibsen returns to the subject so vital to him,—the Social Lie and Duty,—this time as manifesting themselves in the sacred institution of the home and in the position of woman in her gilded cage.

Nora is the beloved, adored wife of *Torvald Helmer*. He is an admirable man, rigidly honest, of high moral ideals, and passionately devoted to his wife and children. In short, a good man and an enviable husband. Almost every mother would be proud of such a match for her daughter, and the latter would consider herself fortunate to become the wife of such a man.

Nora, too, considers herself fortunate. Indeed, she worships her husband, believes in him implicitly, and is sure that if ever her safety should be menaced, *Torvald*, her idol, her god, would perform the miracle....

...then...she realizes how much she has been wronged, that she is only a plaything, a doll to *Helmer*. In her disillusionment she says, "You have never loved me. You only thought it amusing to be in love with me."

Helmer. Why, Nora, what a thing to say!

Nora. Yes, it is so, Torvald. While I was at home with father he used to tell me all his opinions and I held the same opinions. If I had others I concealed them, because he would not have liked it. He used to call me his doll child, and play with me as I played with my dolls. Then I came to live in your house—...I mean I passed from father's hands into yours. You settled everything according to your taste; and I got the same tastes as you; or I pretended to—I don't know which—both ways perhaps. When I look back on it now, I seem to have been living here like a beggar, from hand to mouth. I lived by performing tricks for you, Torvald. But you would have it so. You and father have done me a great wrong. It's your fault that my life has been wasted....

Helmer. It's exasperating! Can you forsake your holiest duties in this way?

Nora. What do you call my holiest duties?

Helmer. Do you ask me that? Your duties to your husband and children.

Nora. I have other duties equally sacred.

Helmer. Impossible! What duties do you mean?

Nora. My duties toward myself.

Helmer. Before all else you are a wife and a mother.

A Doll's House

Nora. That I no longer believe. I think that before all else I am a human being, just as much as you are—or, at least, I will try to become one. I know that most people agree with you, Torvald, and that they say so in books. But henceforth I can't be satisfied with what most people say, and what is in books. I must think things out for myself and try to get clear about them...I had been living here these eight years with a strange man, and had borne him three children—Oh! I can't bear to think of it—I could tear myself to pieces!...I can't spend the night in a strange man's house.

Is there anything more degrading to woman than to live with a stranger, and bear him children? Yet, the lie of the marriage institution decrees that she shall continue to do so, and the social conception of duty insists that for the sake of that lie she need be nothing else than a plaything, a doll, a nonentity.

When *Nora* closes behind her the door of her doll's house, she opens wide the gate of life for woman, and proclaims the revolutionary message that only perfect freedom and communion make a true bond between man and woman, meeting in the open, without lies, without shame, free from the bondage of duty.

Excerpted from *The Social Significance of the Modern Drama* by Emma Goldman (1914)

Document Twenty-Four

Excerpts from Walt Whitman's poetry, published in *Mother Earth*:
"Envy" (*Mother Earth*, May 1906)
"I Sit and Look Out" (*Mother Earth*, August 1916)
From "Leaves of Grass" (*Mother Earth*, March 1917)

Context: Emma Goldman hoped that her magazine would become a political and cultural forum. She introduced her readers to writers and poets whose work expressed the optimism of her belief in social harmony and individual freedom but did not hesitate to give voice to the outrage against the injustices around them. Although poetry is no longer as popular a form of expression, Walt Whitman's poems have remained an emblem of the American belief in individual freedom and democracy. By prominently including Whitman's poetry in her magazine, Goldman hoped to link the American anarchist tradition with the European anarchist tradition. Later in her life, Goldman wrote an essay about Whitman himself, and the ways in which his homosexual identity deepened the meaning of his poetry, and how negative social attitudes about homosexuality prevented him from fully expressing himself.

Questions on the documents:
What themes link these three Whitman poems?
Do you think that Whitman's perspective is optimistic and/or pessimistic about the world he lived in?
What kind of history books and newspaper articles would be written if the authors shared Whitman's perspective on what is fundamental to life?

General Questions:
What kinds of changes do you think must take place in the world to create Whitman's "new city of Friends"? Can a poem be part of the process of change?
How does the power of poetry differ from prose? Does it seem more accessible or less accessible? Why, and in what ways?
What kind of poetry is part of your life? Can you give an example of a contemporary song or rap that speaks to people and social issues in a unique way?

10c. A COPY $1 A YEAR

MOTHER EARTH

Monthly Magazine Devoted to Social Science and Literature

Published Every 15th of the Month

EMMA GOLDMAN, Publisher, P. O. Box 217, Madison Square Station, New York, N. Y.

Vol. I MAY, 1906 No. 3

ENVY.

By WALT WHITMAN.

When I peruse the conquered fame of heroes, and the victories of mighty generals, I do not envy the generals,

Nor the President in his Presidency, nor the rich in his great house;

But when I hear of the brotherhood of lovers, how it was with them,

How through life, through dangers, odium, unchanging, long and rong

Through youth, and through middle and old age, how unfaltering, how affectionate and faithful they were,

Then I am pensive—I hastily walk away, filled with the bitterest envy.

MOTHER EARTH

Monthly Magazine Devoted to Social Science and Literature
Published Every 15th of the Month

EMMA GOLDMAN, Publisher and Editor, 20 East 125th Street, New York, N. Y.

Entered as second-class matter April 9, 1906, at the post office at New York, N. Y., under the Act of Congress of March 3, 1879.

Vol. XI **AUGUST, 1916** **No. 6**

I SIT AND LOOK OUT

By Walt Whitman

I SIT and look upon all the sorrows of the world, and
upon all oppression and shame,
I hear secret convulsive sobs from young men at
anguish with themselves, remorseful after deeds
done,
I see in low life the mother misused by her children, dy-
ing, neglected, gaunt, desperate,
I see the wife misused by her husband, I see the treacher-
ous seducer of young women,
I mark the ranklings of jealousy and unrequited love
attempted to be hid, I see these sights on the earth,
I see the workings of battle, pestilence, tyranny, I see
martyrs and prisoners,
I observe a famine at sea, I observe the sailors casting
lots who shall be kill'd to preserve the lives of the
rest,
I observe the slights and degradations cast by arrogant
persons upon labourers, the poor, and upon negroes,
and the like;
All these—all the meanness and agony without end I
sitting look out upon,
See, hear, and am silent.

MOTHER EARTH

Monthly Magazine Devoted to Social Science and Literature
Published Every 15th of the Month

EMMA GOLDMAN, Publisher and Editor, 20 East 125th Street
New York, N. Y.

Entered as second-class matter April 9, 1906, at the post office at New York, N. Y., under the Act of Congress of March 3, 1879.

Vol. XII **MARCH, 1917** **No. 1**

FROM "LEAVES OF GRASS"

BY WALT WHITMAN

I DREAM'D in a dream I saw a city invincible to the attacks of the whole of the rest of the earth,
I dreamed that was the new city of Friends,
Nothing was greater there than the quality of robust love; it led the rest,
It was seen every hour in the actions of the men of that city,
And in all their looks and words.

* * *

WHAT think you I take my pen in hand to record?
The battle-ship, perfect-modell'd, majestic, that I saw pass the offing to-day under full sail?
The splendours of the past day? or the splendour of the night that envelops me?
Or the vaunted glory and growth of the great city spread around me?—no;
But merely of two simple men I saw to-day on the pier in the midst of the crowd, parting the parting of dear friends,
The one to remain hung on the other's neck and passionately kiss'd him,
While the one to depart tightly prest the one to remain in his arms.

Topic Five: Art and Literature of Social Change
Suggested Activities

What is the purpose of studying the social, political, literary, and artistic changes during the period of Emma Goldman's life (1869-1940)? Find examples of the major artistic and photographic movements of the time and intuit how you think Goldman would have responded to them.

Read a novel (e.g. *All Quiet on the Western Front*, *Bread Givers*, *Sister Carrie*) or short stories from the period and comment on whether they correspond to or contradict Goldman's ideas.

Paint, draw, write, or perform something that might elicit a resolution to a conflict at your school.

Biographical Essay on Emma Goldman

Biographical Essay on Emma Goldman

Emma Goldman was born in the Jewish quarter of a small Russian city in modern Lithuania on June 27, 1869. Her painful recollections of childhood include witnessing violence against women and children, peasants brutalized by landlords, Jews ghettoized and frequently forced to move in search of work, and endless streams of corrupt petty officials extorting fees from a relatively powerless constituency. Her family life was difficult. Goldman's father, whom she referred to as "the nightmare of my childhood," made her the special object of his frequent rages. Her mother, who could plead eloquently and persuasively on behalf of young men about to be drafted into the Russian army, was nonetheless emotionally distant from her children and frequently depressed.

At thirteen, Goldman moved with her family to the Jewish ghetto in St. Petersburg where ideas of revolution filled the air. The Russian populists and nihilists sparked Goldman's imagination and reinforced her faith that injustice could and must be confronted. An avid reader, Goldman devoured forbidden novels and political tracts and found role models in the young women of the revolution. Goldman desperately wanted to help create a new world of equality, justice, and family harmony.

Goldman's father had no such public vision of his daughter's future, instead he was determined that she marry young and live a conventional life. His attempts to secure her engagement at age fifteen precipitated her flight from home. She and her older sister fled Russia for America. Full of optimism, Goldman entered a new country where she assumed that she had escaped the traditional barriers to women's freedom so pervasive in the old world. She settled with relatives in 1885 in Rochester, New York. Sadly she discovered that family life in the Jewish ghetto of Rochester and piecework in the textile factory did not differ significantly from what she had left behind in Russia. Asserting her new freedom in intimate life in America, Goldman soon fell in love with a co-worker and chose to marry him.

In 1886, a shocking political event changed her life. To protest the brutal suppression of a strike at the McCormick Harvester Company, labor and radical activists held a mass rally in Chicago's Haymarket Square. A bomb exploded, killing seven police officers and injuring many protestors in the crowd. Anarchist leaders were blamed for the incident. Tried on flimsy evidence, four of the accused were sentenced to death and executed. When Goldman learned of the political trial and conviction of the anarchists, she immediately recognized the similarity between their ideas and those of the Russian populists. She began reading everything she could find on anarchism. Goldman consciously decided to devote her life to the ideal of anarchism to prove that the message of the Haymarket martyrs had not died with them.

With the crystallization of Goldman's political ideas came changes in her personal life. Risking the stigma of divorce, Goldman left her husband and headed for a new life, first in New Haven, then in New York City. Within a year she was living in a commune with other Russian-born anarchists, including her first great love and eventual life-long comrade, Alexander Berkman. The twenty-year-old idealist soon became a prominent member of New York City's immigrant anarchist community.

Her newfound stability was undermined in 1892 when Henry Clay Frick of the Carnegie Steel Company provoked a bloody confrontation with workers during a strike at Carnegie's plant in Homestead, Pennsylvania. Berkman and Goldman decided to retaliate; Berkman went to Homestead to shoot Frick to demonstrate to the world that violence begets violence and that workers would no longer accept the brutality of the capitalist factory owners. The act backfired; Berkman wounded Frick but did not kill him; he served a fourteen-year prison term, not as a hero of the working class but rather as the catalyst for the resurgence of nationwide fear of anarchists. Insufficient evidence of collaboration in the attempt on Frick's life allowed Goldman to escape indictment, but her widely known intimate association with Berkman inspired the press to sensationalize its portrayal of "Red Emma" as the fearsome demon of unharnessed sexuality and violence.

This violent image was reinforced in 1901 when President William McKinley was assassinated by Leon Czolgosz, who claimed to be an anarchist acting under Goldman's influence. Although she did not know the young man who evidently had attended one of her lectures, she was immediately arrested as an accomplice to the crime. The stigma of this association was so great that even after she was set free for lack of evidence against her, it was several years before she could safely appear in public under her own name. Even so, she tempted the fates by continuing to address select meetings. By the time she re-emerged fully, her lectures were prefaced by a disavowal of the efficacy of the tactics of individual acts of political violence—with one caveat to the public: she asked them to resist the inclination to abandon political prisoners whose tactics may differ from their own. Based on her growing conviction that "the most violent element in society is ignorance," she founded a political and literary magazine, *Mother Earth*, which ran from 1906 to 1917. It was not only a forum for anarchist ideas and news of international movements but also an opportunity to publish poetry and drama criticism. It introduced its subscribers to dramatists like Ibsen, Strindberg, and Shaw, and to political cartoonists and artists like Man Ray. The magazine's circulation was not limited to the United States. Gradually its influence and readership spread to Europe as Goldman's international reputation grew.

Goldman expanded her audience in the United States through national lecture tours on behalf of the magazine. For almost ten years, from 1908 until 1917, she was assisted in her tours by an amorous and flamboyant road manager, Dr. Ben Reitman. Emma and Ben crisscrossed the country, appearing before ever widening audiences, curious about Goldman's political and social challenge and appreciative of the support she gave to each locality's current labor and political battles. On their 1910 tour, for example, Goldman spoke 120 times in thirty-seven cities in twenty-five states to 25,000 people.

Her talks were varied and expansive. It was not unusual for Goldman to speak on "The Intermediate Sex: A Discussion of Homosexuality" one night and "The Social Value of Modern Drama" the next. Appreciating literature and drama as powerful vehicles for awakening social change, particularly on sex and gender issues, Goldman welcomed the challenge of alerting and educating the American public to the importance of modern European and Russian drama. She believed that education was a lifelong process and that public schools often excluded open-ended discussions and provocative challenges to the *status quo* from the curriculum. As a proponent of the Modern School movement which fostered independence and creativity, she often asserted that a state-run school "is for the child what the prison is for the convict and the barracks for the soldier—a place where everything is being used to break the will of the child, and then to pound, knead, and shape it into a being utterly foreign to itself."

This belief in the importance of widening the experience of the individual had specific ramifications for women. Goldman will be remembered for her pioneering work for the liberation of women, identifying birth control as an essential element in the larger battle for women's sexual and economic freedom. Goldman believed that the law that denied women access to birth control information was symptomatic of general social and economic injustice as well as the particular oppression of women. She was a political mentor to the young Margaret Sanger, though Sanger eventually parted ways with Goldman and shifted her focus to the single, more pragmatic goal of winning the legal right to distribute birth control information. Goldman continued to insist that the battle for woman's control over her body should be part of a broader struggle against the social, economic, and political conditions that fostered and reinforced inequality.

This was not the only time Goldman broke with the other feminists of her day; she criticized the women's suffrage movement for its claim that the vote was the best vehicle to secure the equality of women, pointing out that it would not adequately address the issue of the liberation of working-class women, nor ensure a gentler form of government.

Goldman spoke eloquently on the political dimension of personal life, and women, from within and outside of the suffrage movement, crowded into Goldman's lectures. Of particular interest was her lecture on "Marriage and Love" in which she articulated the liberating potential of free love in contrast to the stifling aspects of marriage for women. As an anarchist, she hoped to be the living example of her ideal. Yet privately she agonized over whether her own failure in love made her unworthy of delivering this message. Throughout her ten-year love affair with her road manager Ben Reitman, her passionate letters reveal dark feelings of jealousy written at the same time she spoke eloquently on the platform about the corrosive effect of possessiveness in love; similarly she wrote to Ben with a longing for security and rest, just as she became the symbol and the harbinger of the total independence of women. Her inner doubts and anguish prompted her to write to Ben that if she remained "an abject slave to her love" she would stand "condemned before the bar of [her] own reason."

Goldman's eloquence on the themes of personal life as they related to political and social forces was in part the key to her popularity. Threatened by her anarchist politics, her persuasive powers, and her discussion of topics often considered taboo, the police and local authorities frequently banned her lectures. Inevitably a debate over the rights of free speech would follow. Goldman's relentless assertion of the critical importance of the right to freedom of speech in a democratic society ultimately blazed the trail for the enforcement of First Amendment rights in America. Braving the mounting obstacles to free speech, Goldman paid dearly for her principles. Under surveillance most of her adult life, she was arrested and jailed countless times and spent her last eighteen months in the United States imprisoned on federal charges.

Her longest jail sentence was the direct result of her organizing efforts against the involuntary conscription of young men into the military. Within weeks of America's entry into World War I, Goldman and her old friend Alexander Berkman helped launch the No-Conscription League to educate and encourage conscientious objection to the war. In the past, Goldman had condemned U.S. expansionism during the Spanish-American War and denounced British imperialism during the Boer War, but the patriotic fervor surrounding World War I bred a more severe intolerance for dissent, considering such opposition to war a "clear and present danger" to the nation. The government had Berkman and Goldman arrested on the charge of conspiracy against the draft. They were convicted and sentenced to two years in prison with the possibility of deportation upon their release.

Alarmed by the post-World War I labor turbulence and by recurring bombing incidents, the Wilson administration retaliated against the most vulnerable radical and progressive organizations. Just after her release from prison on September 27, 1919, Goldman was re-arrested by the young

J. Edgar Hoover, director of the Justice Department's General Intelligence Division. Writing the briefs and building the case against Goldman himself, Hoover quietly worked behind the scenes to persuade the courts to deny her citizenship claims and to deport her. On December 21, 1919, Goldman, Berkman, and 247 other foreign-born radicals were herded aboard the S.S. *Buford* and sent to the Soviet Union.

With the exception of a brief ninety-day lecture tour in 1934, Emma Goldman spent the remaining twenty-one years of her life in exile from the United States. During this period she lived in Russia, Sweden, Germany, France, England, Spain, and Canada, never finding a political "home" outside the United States.

In no country did Emma Goldman feel more estranged than in her native Russia. She was shocked by the ruthless authoritarianism of the Bolshevik regime, its severe repression of anarchists, and its disregard for individual freedom. Among the first vocal opponents on the left to criticize the Soviet Union, she alienated many of her peers in Europe and America. In a face-to-face meeting with Lenin in 1920 she questioned the Soviet leader on the lack of freedom of speech and the press in Soviet Russia. Disillusioned with the direction of the revolution, Goldman and Berkman eventually left Russia.

Exiled, wandering from country to country, Goldman felt constrained and often depressed. In the 1920s and 1930s, while struggling to survive economically, she engaged in a variety of literary projects. The most enduring product of this period of self-reflection is her moving, one-thousand-page autobiography, *Living My Life* (1931).

Goldman was sixty-seven years old when the Spanish Civil War erupted in July of 1936. The promise of an anarchist revolution in Spain revived her broken spirits. When Spanish comrades asked Goldman to direct their English propaganda campaign, she visited collectivized towns and farms in Aragon and the Levante and was electrified by what seemed to her to be the beginnings of a true anarchist revolution. Dismayed but not vanquished by Franco's triumph in early 1939, Goldman moved to Canada where she devoted the last year of her life to securing political asylum for women and children refugees of the Spanish war, publicizing legislative dangers to free speech in Canada, and campaigning on behalf of foreign-born radicals threatened with deportation to fascist countries.

After Goldman's death on May 14, 1940, the U.S. Immigration and Naturalization Service allowed her body to be readmitted to the United States. She is buried in Waldheim Cemetery, Chicago, near the Haymarket anarchists who so inspired her.

Glossary

Glossary

Anarchism: Anarchism is the political philosophy of those who believe that a society based on shared ownership and voluntary agreements among individuals and groups is possible and that without each person's consent and involvement in the social order all established forms of government essentially rest upon the threat of force. As a result, some anarchists believed in the use of violence to bring about change. Emma Goldman, however, believed that social change would occur only when people's beliefs and attitudes changed, and hence her lectures were intended to educate and to inspire her audiences with a vision of social harmony. She identified with the anti-authoritarian tradition of writers Henry David Thoreau, Walt Whitman, and Leo Tolstoy as well as prominent anarchist political theorists like Peter Kropotkin and Michael Bakunin.

Bolsheviks: Led by V. I. Lenin, the Bolsheviks were a centralized, disciplined party of professional revolutionaries. They dedicated themselves to overthrowing the Czar—the emperor of Russia—and to the establishment of a classless society. After their successful revolution in November 1917, however, the Bolsheviks were often ruthless toward those they considered enemies of the revolution, including many groups who had fought for decades against Czarist rule and in support of a revolution. Emma Goldman, an early supporter of the revolution, was especially troubled by the Bolsheviks' suppression of free speech and the political activities of the Russian anarchists.

Conscription: Conscription is a government-initiated system for requiring men to serve in the military. Since ancient times governments have conscripted men when they needed an army. During World Wars I and II, the Korean War, and the Vietnam War, the U.S. government used a form of conscription called the draft, which excused some individuals from military service if, for example, they were employed in war-related industries or engaged in higher education or were "conscientious objectors"—opposed to war on a moral level and willing to participate in alternative service. The draft has often been a source of controversy in the United States. When the federal government began registering men for the draft during the Civil War, four days of rioting in New York City claimed the lives of over one hundred people. Those opposed to the Vietnam War often expressed their opposition by refusing to register for the draft or by burning their draft cards. Goldman and thousands of other liberals and radicals opposed conscription during World War I. Goldman was charged with conspiracy to obstruct the draft because she believed that it violated an individual's right to choose whether or not to fight. She was found guilty and sentenced to two years in jail. Since 1973 the American military has been a volunteer force, though all males are required to register for a standby draft when they reach the age of eighteen.

Comstock Law: In 1873 Anthony Comstock, organizer of the New York Society for the Suppression of Vice, successfully lobbied Congress for passage of a law to bar "obscene, lewd or lascivious" material from the mails, specifically contraceptives and birth control information. In 1900, after attending a conference in Paris on how to prevent pregnancy, Goldman smuggled contraceptive devices and birth control literature into the United States. Demands for birth control became stronger in the second decade of the century as growing numbers of women and men began to write and lecture on the topic and distribute literature. Margaret Sanger, the most prominent advocate of birth control, was prosecuted under the Comstock law in 1914 when her journal, *Woman Rebel*, addressed the issue of birth control. The Comstock law continued to be used in federal courts as late as the 1950s to prosecute obscenity cases.

Czarist Russia: Before the 1917 revolution, Russia was a monarchy under the rule of the czar, or tsar—the title used by the emperors of Russia. The first ruler to adopt the title was Ivan the Terrible in 1547. The last czar was Nicholas II (1868-1918). Goldman grew up under czarist rule and rebelled against its oppressive nature.

Direct Action: Those who believe that conventional methods to achieve social and political change are slow and inadequate often rely on direct action, a political tactic of confrontation and sometimes illegal disruption intended to attract and arouse public awareness and action. Goldman used the tactic of direct action, for example, when she risked arrest by speaking on birth control before a public gathering. A more recent example of the use of direct action is the civil rights movement in the South in the 1950s and 1960s. In 1955, for example, African Americans refused to ride buses for over a year in Montgomery, Alabama, in a successful effort to have the seating desegregated. And in numerous southern towns and cities African-American college students staged successful "sit ins" to desegregate lunch counters where previously they had been refused service.

Espionage and Sedition Acts of 1917-1918: President Woodrow Wilson's decision to take the United States into World War I was not welcomed by everybody in this country. Pacifists, isolationists, socialists and other radicals were politically opposed to U.S. entry into the war, and considerable numbers of German Americans and Irish Americans also opposed U.S. involvement, though for different reasons. German Americans did not want the United States at war with their homeland and Irish Americans opposed the U.S. allying with Great Britain, which held their homeland in colonial bondage. The Espionage Act of June 1917 imposed fines of up to $10,000 and prison terms of up to twenty years on anyone found guilty of interfering with the nation's war effort, obstructing recruitment, or promoting disloyalty. Under another provision of the Act the postmaster general was allowed to prohibit the use of the mails for any material "advocating or urging treason, insurrection, or forcible resistance to any law of the United States." The Act was directed at opponents of the war rather than those who actually intended to engage in "espionage." Even though the Act violated First Amendment rights of freedom of expression, the government argued that the prohibited activity presented a "clear and present danger" to a nation at war. The Justice Department convicted over a thousand individuals under its provisions, including the leaders of the Industrial Workers of the World and the Socialist party leader, Eugene Debs. Another law, the Sedition Act of May 1918 gave the government more power over expressions of dissent. It prohibited "uttering, printing, writing, or publishing any disloyal, profane, scurrilous, or abusive language ... [about] ... the form of government of the United States, or the Constitution, or the flag" or urging slowdown of production of anything necessary to the war effort.

Haymarket Incident: On May 3, 1886, during a strike at the McCormick Reaper Works, the police shot at random at the strikers who were demanding an eight-hour work day. A mass meeting was called by a Chicago anarchist group for the following evening to protest the police shooting. As the peaceful meeting in Haymarket Square was drawing to a close, police began to break up the gathering. At that point a bomb was thrown at the police, who, in turn, opened fire. Seven police officers and several civilians were killed. The police and the newspapers blamed Chicago's anarchist leaders for the incident, and eight of them were arrested. In a climate of unusual fear of radicals a jury found them guilty of murder. Of the eight convicted, four were executed, one committed suicide, and three were sentenced to long prison terms but were later pardoned. Emma Goldman, who was seventeen years old at the time, closely followed the fate of the Haymarket anarchists. She was deeply moved by their commitment to their cause and the injustice done to them. When they were executed she determined to devote her life to their ideal and memory, recalling later that "their death was my spiritual birth."

Homestead Strike: In 1892, the union contract between skilled workers at the Homestead (Pennsylvania) Works and the Carnegie Steel Company was due to expire. Henry Clay Frick, the superintendent at Homestead and an outspoken anti-union man, proposed a new pay scale that cut workers' wages by 20 percent. On June 29, the workers called for a strike to protest Frick's proposal. Before they began the strike, however, Frick locked them out, imported a force of three hundred Pinkerton detectives, and began recruiting replacement workers. A violent battle between the locked-out workers and Pinkerton agents left three detectives and nine strikers dead. The Governor of Pennsylvania ordered in the National Guard. Into this conflict came Alexander Berkman, Emma Goldman's comrade, who saw himself as the self-appointed avenger of the dead workers and the wrongs suffered by all the workers. On July 23 he entered Frick's office and shot and stabbed him several times. Frick survived the attack; Berkman, seized on the spot, was tried and found guilty by a jury and spent fourteen years in jail. Ironically, the Homestead workers actually condemned Berkman's act as ineffective; Goldman, who had helped plan the attempt on Frick's life, stood by her friend during his long imprisonment. Later, Goldman rejected violence as a tactic but refused to condemn those like Berkman who risked their lives for their ideal. Ultimately, Goldman believed that the violence done to individuals by the economic and political system was more destructive than such individual acts of violence.

Industrial Workers of the World (IWW): Emma Goldman had close ties to the leaders of the IWW. Founded in 1905, the IWW (or Wobblies, as they were known) tried to organize all workers, regardless of their craft or level of skill, into one large union. This approach put the IWW in direct conflict with the American Federation of Labor (AFL). AFL unions restricted membership to skilled workers such as carpenters, typographers, glassblowers, and boilermakers. The IWW's goals and tactics were also different: the IWW wanted its members to seize control of the factories and mines and often employed the tactics of direct action, while the AFL fought mainly for better wages and working conditions for its members within the system of industrial capitalism. The IWW kept its dues low as part of a strategy to recruit the broadest range of unskilled immigrants, women, nonwhites, and migrant workers. Its newspapers were lively—and included publications in numerous foreign languages—and its songs and pictures have become legendary. Where local authorities prevented Wobblies from recruiting members the IWW often had to wage "free speech fights," calling members across the nation to descend on a city where they had been denied the right to speak on the streets and distribute literature. No matter how many Wobblies were arrested, there were more to take their places, and eventually the local authorities had to give up. But the IWW's most dramatic confrontations came in the strikes it organized, such as the textile workers strike in Lawrence, Massachusetts (1912) and the Paterson silk strike (1913). Later, many Wobblies were vocal opponents of WWI and conscription. They fell victim to wartime anti-radical hysteria—in September 1917 Justice Department agents raided IWW offices across the country, arresting virtually all of its leadership. Over one hundred of them were found guilty of violating the Espionage Act, and many were sentenced to long jail terms. The IWW never recovered from this blow.

Jingoism: the term is generally negative and applies to extreme patriotism used especially to persuade public opinion in support of war.

McKinley Assassination: William McKinley (Republican), elected president of the United States in 1896 and 1900, was shot by an assassin while attending the Pan-American Exposition in

Buffalo, New York, on September 6, 1901. Eight days later McKinley died from his wounds. His assassin, Leon Czolgosz, a twenty-eight-year-old unemployed laborer and anarchist, was apprehended at the scene. The nation's newspapers were filled with detailed reports of the crime, and many implicated Emma Goldman in the act. Some reported that Czolgosz had heard Goldman speak; others claimed a copy of a Goldman lecture was found in his pocket when the police searched him. The authorities interrogated Goldman, but no evidence was uncovered to prove that she had any connection to the crime, though she was forever associated in the public mind with McKinley's assassination.

Palmer Raids: In the United States, World War I created a climate of intolerance and suspicion of radicals and war resisters that continued even after the war ended. The success of the Bolshevik revolution in Russia only served to increase the fear of radicalism and suspicion of foreigners. The Palmer raids—part of the postwar "Red Scare"—specifically targeted foreign-born radicals. Beginning in January 1920, under the direction of Attorney General A. Mitchell Palmer, agents of the Justice Department raided offices and homes, arresting thousands of people—often without warrants—destroying property, and conducting unlawful searches. These violations of constitutional guarantees alarmed many Americans, who worried that the wholesale trampling of civil liberties set a disturbing example. It is no coincidence that the American Civil Liberties Union was founded in the same year as the Palmer raids occurred.

Preparedness: From the beginning of World War I some prominent Americans, including former President Theodore Roosevelt and Senator Henry Cabot Lodge, were eager to join the war against Germany. They pressured President Woodrow Wilson to enlarge and improve America's armed forces. But Wilson initially sought to avoid U.S. involvement in the war, attempting instead to find peace terms acceptable to both sides. After his attempts to promote peace were rejected the president began a campaign of preparedness that involved enlargement of the army, navy, and marines. Wilson campaigned for reelection in 1916 on the slogan, "He kept us out of war," but many Americans believed that his preparedness program would inevitably lead to U.S. entry into the war. Emma Goldman and others denounced this military build-up. After the United States entered the war in April 1917, they encouraged Americans to oppose the war by refusing forced conscription (involuntary drafting of young men) into the military.

Radicals: "Radical" is from the Latin word "radix," which means root. Radicals are activists who look for the roots of the social, economic, and political wrongs in society and demand immediate and sweeping changes to remedy them.

Selected Resources

Recommended Films and Videos

The following films are recommended as the most relevant to the study of Emma Goldman and the issues of importance during her lifetime. Check your local school or public library—many school systems may already have these films in their media libraries. Public libraries also have extensive film and video collections.

"The Wobblies" (1979)
Directed by Stewart Bird and Deborah Shaffer — 89 minutes, color

From 1905 to World War I, members of the Industrial Workers of the World (IWW), nicknamed the "Wobblies," traveled across the country organizing workers into "One Big Union."

"The Wobblies" integrates the music of the period with newsreel footage and interviews with IWW members. The cultural, political, and legal events of the time are carefully documented, creating an extraordinary record of one of the most exciting periods in American labor history.

Distributor: First Run/Icarus Films
153 Waverly Place
New York, NY 10014
(212) 727-1711

Sale:	16 mm	$1,350
	1/2" video	700
Rental:	16 mm	150

"The Good Fight: The Abraham Lincoln Brigade in the Spanish Civil War" (1984)
Directed by Noel Buckner, Mary Dore, and Sam Sills — 98 minutes, color

Under the banner of the Abraham Lincoln Brigade, 3,200 Americans joined forces with volunteers from around the world to fight against Franco and the rise of fascism in Spain.

Interviews with eleven veterans of the Spanish Civil War reveal in deeply personal terms why they joined this struggle. The newsreel footage and songs of the resistance help to make this film an inspirational look at the "conscience of the thirties." It is important to note that this film focuses on the American experience in Spain, mostly from the point of view of Communist party members, not the anarchists who believed that they were not only fighting in a civil war, but also for a Spanish revolution.

Distributor: First Run/Icarus Films
153 Waverly Place
New York, NY 10014
(212) 727-1711

Sale:	16mm	$1,350
	video	675
Rental:	16mm	150

"Reds" (1981)
Directed by Warren Beatty, Paramount Films (Rated PG) — 199 minutes, color
Starring Warren Beatty, Diane Keaton, Maureen Stapleton, Jack Nicholson

A sweeping epic of revolution and political idealism, "Reds" is the story of writer John Reed and his journalist wife Louise Bryant, whose radical ideas and passion are brought to life in this gripping feature film. Emma Goldman, played by Maureen Stapleton, figures prominently in this Oscar-winning film. Based on historian Robert Rosenstone's biography of John Reed, *Romantic Revolutionary* (New York: Alfred A. Knopf, 1975).

Available at most video rental stores.

"Anarchism in America"
Directed by Steven Fischler and Joel Sucher — 75 minutes, color

This feature length documentary weaves rare archival footage with on-camera interviews to present a broad survey of anarchist history and thought in America, and contains newsreel footage of Emma Goldman dating from her ninety-day U.S. lecture tour in 1934. Anarchism's origins are examined both as a foreign ideology brought to America by immigrants such as Emma Goldman and Sacco and Vanzetti and as a native philosophy stemming from nineteenth-century individualism. The film also explores the relationship of anarchist influences on the anti-nuclear movement and the anti-Vietnam War era.

Distributor: The Cinema Guild
1697 Broadway
New York, NY 10019
(212) 246-5522

Sale:	16mm	$1,000
	video	695
Rental:	16mm	100

The Secret Intelligence—Episode #1: "The Only Rule is Win" (1988)
Written by Blaine Baggett and Arthur Barron — 60 minutes, color

This is the first episode in a series produced by the Public Broadcasting System about the history and development of the Central Intelligence Agency. It traces the early career of J. Edgar Hoover and his ambitious efforts to rid the United States of "foreign radicals" including Emma Goldman. This is a well-researched presentation that includes excellent archival footage, including an unidentified fleeting glance of Emma Goldman's deportation in 1919.

Distributor: PBS Video
1320 Braddock Place
Alexandria, VA 22314-1698
1 (800) 238-7271

Sale: video $59.95

"Free Voice of Labor: The Jewish Anarchists" (1980)
Directed by Steven Fischler and Joel Sucher — 55 minutes, color

The lives and ideals of the people involved with the publication of the Jewish anarchist newspaper, *Freie Arbeiter Stimme* (Free Voice of Labor), are presented through on-camera interviews interwoven with clips from the Yiddish cinema and rare archival news footage. Yiddish "songs of struggle" are an integral part of this wonderful documentary that captures the spirit and idealism of a generation committed to social change.

Distributed by: Cinema Guild
1697 Broadway
New York, NY 10019
(212) 246-5522

Sale:	16mm	$895
	video	595
Rental:	16mm	95
	video	95

Selected Bibliography

WORKS BY GOLDMAN and CONTEMPORARY EDITIONS OF PRIMARY SOURCES

Goldman, Emma. ***Living My Life***. 2 vols. New York: Alfred A. Knopf, 1931. Reprint. 2 vols. New York: Dover Publications, 1970 (still in print). Reprint. In one volume. Salt Lake City: Gibbs M. Smith, Inc., 1982. The three editions above have the same pagination.
Abridged ed. New York: New American Library, 1977. Edited by Richard and Anna Maria Drinnon.

Goldman's thousand-page autobiography, the best overview of her early life and political involvement in the United States, covers her life to her deportation in 1919 to Soviet Russia and her exile in Europe and Canada. Indexed for easy reference.

Mother Earth. Reprint. New York: Greenwood Reprint Corporation, 1968.

The radical periodical that Goldman edited and published between 1906 and 1917 includes reports on her lecture tours; articles on political, social, and cultural issues; poetry; and political art on the cover of each issue. Among the writers who appeared in *Mother Earth* were Peter Kropotkin, Voltairine de Cleyre, Francisco Ferrer, Alexander Berkman, and, of course, Emma Goldman. *Mother Earth* also reprinted essays by writers such as Leo Tolstoy and Friedrich Nietzsche.

Goldman, Emma. ***Anarchism and Other Essays***. New York: Mother Earth Publishing Association, 1910. Reprint. New York: Dover Publications, 1969 (still in print).

A collection of Goldman's earliest essays that includes her discussion of the theory and practice of anarchism, plus "Patriotism: A Menace to Liberty," "The Tragedy of Woman's Emancipation," and "The Drama: A Powerful Disseminator of Radical Thought"—all written in Goldman's own forthright style.

Goldman, Emma. ***My Disillusionment in Russia.*** London: C. W. Daniel Co., 1925 (complete text). Reprint. New York: Thomas Y. Crowell Company, Apollo Editions, 1970. Reprint. Gloucester, Mass.: Peter Smith, 1983.

This compelling 250-page book recounts Goldman's experiences in Soviet Russia in 1920-21 and is especially timely for the advanced high school student of history. Includes Goldman's analysis of the Russian Revolution and the Bolsheviks' suppression of free speech and especially the organizing activities of the anarchists.

Goldman, Emma. ***The Social Significance of the Modern Drama.*** Boston: Richard G. Badger, 1914. Reprint. New York: Applause Theatre Book Publishers, 1987.

Demonstrates Goldman's belief in the transformational power of modern drama, focusing on Scandinavian, German, French, English, Irish, and Russian playwrights such as Ibsen, Strindberg, Hauptmann, Shaw, and Chekhov.

Drinnon, Richard and Anna Maria, eds. ***Nowhere at Home: Letters from Exile of Emma Goldman and Alexander Berkman.*** New York: Schocken Books, 1975.

A moving collection of letters between lifelong friends and comrades written in middle and old age after they were expelled from the United States. The book is arranged in chapters under subjects such as "Communism and the Intellectuals," "Anarchism and Violence," and "Women and Men." An introduction, autobiographical fragment, and chronology complement these letters for the advanced high school reader.

Shulman, Alix Kates, ed. ***Red Emma Speaks: Selected Writings and Speeches by Emma Goldman.*** New York: Random House, 1972. Reprint. New York: Schocken Books, 1982.

An important collection of Goldman's essays and speeches drawn from the entire span of her career, arranged in four sections, "Organization of Society," "Social Institutions," "Violence," and "Two Revolutions and a Summary."

BIOGRAPHY

Chalberg, John. ***Emma Goldman: American Individualist.*** New York: HarperCollins Publishers, 1991.

A brief (180-page) biography of Goldman's life from her emigration from Czarist Russia through her career in the United States to her life in exile. Appropriate for junior high and high school readers.

Drinnon, Richard. ***Rebel in Paradise: A Biography of Emma Goldman.*** Chicago: University of Chicago Press, 1961. Reprint. Boston: Beacon Press, 1970. Reprint. New York: Harper & Row, 1976.

Approximately 300-page biography of Goldman suitable for the advanced high school reader. Chronicles Goldman's entire life with a focus on her contribution to the movement for free speech. All editions include illustrations and photographs of Goldman and her comrades .

Falk, Candace. ***Love, Anarchy, and Emma Goldman.*** New York: Holt, Rinehart and Winston, 1984. Rev. ed. New Brunswick, N.J.: Rutgers University Press, 1990.

Complete biography of Goldman with an emphasis on the connection between her public vision and the realities of her private intimate life. A good way for the student to find many of the issues of love, jealousy, and women's struggle for independence mirrored and then brought out of the personal into the political realm, thus fostering an engagement with history.

Morton, Marian J. ***Emma Goldman and the American Left: "Nowhere at Home".*** New York: Twayne Publishers, 1992.

A brief biography of Goldman that relies heavily on published sources, especially ***Living My Life,*** and is suitable for high school students.

Shulman, Alix. ***To The Barricades: The Anarchist Life of Emma Goldman.*** New York: Thomas Y. Crowell Company, 1971.

A well-written biography in the "Women of America" series suitable for junior high students, it concentrates on Goldman's life and career in the United States and includes only thirty pages on her years of exile. Includes an excellent selection of photographs.

Waldstreicher, David. ***Emma Goldman.*** New York: Chelsea House Publishers, 1990.

Part of the "American Women of Achievement" series, this biography is written for junior high students and features many photographs and illustrations. It can be used as a reference or supplemental history text or as a brief introduction to Goldman's life.

AUTOBIOGRAPHIES OF GOLDMAN CONTEMPORARIES

Anderson, Margaret. ***My Thirty Years War: An Autobiography.*** New York: Covici, Friede, 1930. Reprint. Westport, Conn.: Greenwood Press, 1971.

This 270-page autobiography by the editor of the magazine, the *Little Review*, is appropriate for junior or senior high school students. Anderson's impressions of Emma Goldman are documented in the chapter, "The Little Review," and many pictures of their contemporaries accompany the text.

Flynn, Elizabeth Gurley. ***The Rebel Girl: An Autobiography: My First Life (1906-1926).*** New York: International Publishers, 1976. Rev. ed. of ***I Speak My Own Piece: Autobiography of "The Rebel Girl".*** New York: Masses and Mainstream, 1955.

This 350-page autobiography by the famous Industrial Workers of the World agitator and free speech fighter is suitable for high school students and includes photographs and reproductions of original documents. It covers the period from Flynn's childhood to her battles in the Sacco and Vanzetti case during the 1920s.

Sanger, Margaret. ***Margaret Sanger: An Autobiography.*** New York: W. W. Norton, 1938. Reprint. New York: Dover Publications, 1971.

Five hundred pages of advanced high school reading about this birth control pioneer's life from her New York childhood through her tours of Russia, Europe, and finally India in 1936. Sanger's impressions of Goldman are documented in the chapter, "Hear Me for My Cause."

BIOGRAPHIES OF GOLDMAN CONTEMPORARIES

Bruns, Roger A. ***The Damndest Radical: The Life and World of Ben Reitman.*** Urbana: University of Illinois Press, 1987.

A highly readable biography of the flamboyant Ben Reitman, Goldman's manager and lover between 1908 and 1917. This book discusses their work together, their conflicts with authorities across the country, and their tumultuous personal lives. It also chronicles

Reitman's work with hobos, and his activities in promoting public awareness in the prevention of syphilis. Very accessible for high school readers.

Homer, William. ***Robert Henri and His Circle***. Ithaca, N.Y.: Cornell University Press, 1969.

Robert Henri, a painter and teacher at the Ferrer Modern School, was a devoted admirer of Emma Goldman. Henri's interesting insights into Goldman's writings are expressed in the chapter, "Aspects of Henri's Career." A good reference for high school students.

Humphrey, Robert E. ***Children of Fantasy: The First Rebels of Greenwich Village***. New York: John Wiley & Sons, 1978.

Excellent reference for the advanced high school student about the radical movement in Greenwich Village from 1910 to 1920. Hutchins Hapgood, Max Eastman, John Reed, Floyd Dell, Emma Goldman, and others are discussed and appear in many of the photographs.

Powers, Richard Gid. ***Secrecy and Power: The Life of J. Edgar Hoover***. New York: Free Press, 1987.

An excellent biography of the first director of the FBI who served in that position for nearly fifty years. Before assuming that position in 1924, as a Justice Department official, Hoover had taken a personal interest in having Emma Goldman deported. See especially chapter 3, "The Red Years: The Lessons of Success." Suitable for the advanced high school student.

Theoharis, Athan, and John Stuart Cox. ***The Boss: J. Edgar Hoover and the Great American Inquisition***. Philadelphia: Temple University Press, 1988.

Chapter 3, "Emma Goldman and the Scourge of the Infidel," is a fascinating analysis of Hoover's attitude toward the radicals of the World War I era. A good reference for high school students and teachers.

LITERATURE

Cahan, Abraham. ***The Rise of David Levinsky***. New York: Harper & Brothers, 1917. Reprint. New York: Harper, 1960.

This historical novel about one immigrant's assimilation and success on New York's Lower East Side paints a vivid picture of the garment district, the sweat shops, and the rise of the unions. Five hundred thirty pages of easy high school reading.

Day, Douglas. ***The Prison Notebooks of Ricardo Flores Magón***. New York: Harcourt Brace Jovanovich, 1991.

Emma Goldman was an avid supporter of Ricardo Flores Magón and his brother, Enrique, Mexican revolutionaries expelled from their own country at the turn of the century for their political activities against the Mexican dictator, Porfirio Díaz. In the United States, the Magón brothers continued to work in support of the Mexican revolution. Convicted under the Espionage Act for his vocal opposition to World War I, Ricardo died in prison under suspicious circumstances in 1922. This novel, largely, though not entirely, based on historical fact (Magón did not leave behind any prison notebooks), covers the last two months of his life, when he was imprisoned in Leavenworth Penitentiary, Kansas. Day's unromantic reconstruction of history portrays Magón and larger-than-life figures like Pancho Villa and Emiliano Zapata as real people, their idealism coupled with human foibles and character flaws. Includes some vulgar language. For the advanced high school reader.

Duberman, Martin. ***Mother Earth: An Epic Drama of Emma Goldman's Life***. New York: St. Martin's Press, 1991.

Written by a historian, this three-act play captures the intensity of Goldman's (and her comrade, Alexander Berkman's) devotion to their beliefs. Largely faithful to the historical record, the play is suitable for high school literature and history classes.

Gold, Michael. ***Jews Without Money***. New York: H. Liveright, 1930. Reprint. New York: Avon Books, 1965, 1972.

This novel about a boy growing to manhood on the Lower East Side of New York in the late nineteenth and early twentieth centuries is largely autobiographical and captures the flavor of that time and place. Gold was the leading literary figure in the American Communist party when he wrote this novel, and one of the few Communists who remained on good terms with Goldman despite the issues on which they disagreed.

Mannin, Ethel. ***Red Rose: A Novel Based on the Life of Emma Goldman***. London: Jarrolds, 1941.

A balanced fictional treatment of Goldman written by a friend and fellow worker in the cause of the Spanish anarchists. Mannin, a professional writer, admired and respected Goldman's courage and passion for her ideal, but she was not blind to Goldman's shortcomings.

O'Neill, Eugene. ***The Iceman Cometh***. New York: Random House, 1946. Reprint. New York: Vintage Books, 1957. (Reprinted in many other editions).

Characteristic of an O'Neill play, at issue in ***The Iceman Cometh*** are broad philosophical questions. Advanced high school students will profit from this study of human frailty and self-deception, which includes discussions of socialism and anarchism and features an off-stage character based on Emma Goldman.

Thoreau, Henry David. *Civil Disobedience*. 1849 (under the title "Resistance to Civil Government"). ***The Variorum "Civil Disobedience."*** Edited by Walter Harding. New York: Twayne Publishers, 1967.

Although largely ignored during Thoreau's own lifetime, "Civil Disobedience" has become highly regarded in the literature of American political protest. Written after Thoreau's arrest and overnight stay in jail for refusing to pay his taxes in protest of governmental support of slavery, Thoreau advocated individual disobedience of civil laws when in conflict with moral law and conscience. Thoreau's articulate argument has been cited by many political activists since Goldman's time, including Martin Luther King, Jr., and Mahatma Gandhi.

Thoreau, Henry David. *Walden*. 1854. ***The Variorum "Walden."*** Edited by Walter Harding. New York: Twayne Publishers, 1962.

Representative of Thoreau's attempts to link life experiences with art and literature, ***Walden*** was inspired by Thoreau's two years of living a simple existence in the nature surrounding

Walden pond. A critique of America's materialistic society and a reflection on life, spirituality, and nature, *Walden* is ultimately a meditation on democracy, and in praise of individuals motivated by their own principles, not those dictated by urban industrial society. Accessible for high school students.

Whitman, Walt. ***Leaves of Grass***. First edition, 1855. "World's Classics" edition with an introduction by Jerome Loving. Oxford: Oxford University Press, 1990.

A landmark in the history of American literature, this collection of poems has been a favorite of many generations of free thinkers, including Emma Goldman's, for its exaltation of individual freedom and sexual fulfillment, the spiritual power of nature, and for its reflection of the dignity of the common person. Praised by Ralph Waldo Emerson as "the most extraordinary piece of wit and wisdom that American has yet contributed," students should read Whitman's poetry to understand its contributions to literature and history.

Zinn, Howard. "Emma." In Maxine Klein, Lydia Sargent, and Howard Zinn, ***Playbook***. Boston: South End Press, 1986.

This short drama is ideal for classroom role playing. Use it in its entirety, or focus on Act I, Scene 2: "The Family"; or Act II, Scene 14: "Emma and Reporters."

HISTORICAL BACKGROUND

Anderson, Margaret, ed. ***The Little Review Anthology***. New York: Hermitage House, 1953.

Includes excerpts of letters written from prison by Emma Goldman to Margaret Anderson. Also includes writings of the time by T. S. Eliot, Ezra Pound, Gertrude Stein, William Carlos Williams, and others. A good way for the high school student to become more familiar with the literature and art of the period.

Avrich, Paul. ***The Modern School Movement: Anarchism and Education in the United States***. Princeton: Princeton University Press, 1980.

Excellent high school supplement to American history. The chapter, "Rebels and Artists," meticulously describes the events of an anarchist classroom and includes examples of literary and artistic works produced by students of these classrooms.

Chambers, John Whiteclay, II. ***The Eagle and the Dove: The American Peace Movement and United States Foreign Policy, 1900-1922***. 2d ed. Syracuse: Syracuse University Press, 1991.

This collection of documents, with a long introduction by the editor, presents the debate over America's growing role in world affairs that culminated in involvement in World War I. Featured are the differences between Woodrow Wilson, Theodore Roosevelt, pacifists, radicals, and others over the direction of U.S. policy. Well represented is the prominent part played by women—including Jane Addams, Crystal Eastman, Alice Hamilton, and Lillian Wald—in the peace movement of the period.

Debs, Eugene V. ***Writings and Speeches of Eugene V. Debs.*** Introduction by Arthur M. Schlesinger, Jr. New York: Hermitage Press, 1948.

Founder and president of the American Railway Union, Eugene Debs was a bold and powerful speaker and organizer, and a four-time socialist contender for the U.S. presidency, beginning in 1900. For his unrelenting political activities against big business and as an outspoken opponent of World War I, he spent several stints in jail. His famous 1918 antiwar speech to the Ohio Socialist Party convention in Canton, Ohio, which landed him in jail for violation of the Espionage Act, appears in this volume along with other speeches representative of his socialist perspective. Compelling primary source material for the high school student in search of a deeper understanding of the differing political viewpoints of Goldman's time.

Dubofsky, Melvyn. ***We Shall Be All: A History of the Industrial Workers of the World.*** Chicago: Quadrangle Books, 1969. Reprint. Urbana: University of Illinois Press, 1988.

A comprehensive history of the IWW, which tried to organize workers into one large industrial union, in its heyday from its founding in 1905 through World War I. Goldman counted many of its leaders among her friends and lent her support to many of its activities.

Foner, Jack D. ***Blacks and the Military in American History: A New Perspective.*** New York: Praeger Publishers, 1974.

To fill out the picture of American society during World War I, students will be most interested in chapter 6 of this book, which focuses on the opposing opinions of Black leaders like W.E.B. Du Bois, A. Philip Randolph, and Chandler Owen on black participation in World War I, and the experience of African Americans in the military at that time. This chapter details the impact of racism in the military and American society as a whole. It recounts significant events like the 1917 execution of thirteen black soldiers and life-sentencing of forty-two others stationed at Fort Sam Houston for their accused mutiny and murder of sixteen white people, and the race riots and increased Ku Klux Klan lynchings that led to the staging of the 1919 black-led Silent March in New York City.

Foner, Philip S., ed. ***Fellow Workers and Friends: I.W.W. Free Speech Fights as Told by Participants.*** Westport, Conn.: Greenwood Press, 1981.

Excellent compilation of primary source material that includes a biographical introduction to each participant and timelines to guide the reader. IWW comrades such as Elizabeth Gurley Flynn, John Panzner, C. E. Payne, Ed Nolan, and others tell their side of the free speech fights the Wobblies waged in various cities: Missoula 1909, Spokane 1910, Fresno and San Diego 1911-12, the Dakotas 1912-14, Kansas City 1914, and Everett, Washington, 1916. High school history classes may be interested in discovering events in their own city.

Gallo, Marcia, ed. ***Express Yourself: The First Amendment.*** Howard A. Friedman First Amendment Education Project, American Civil Liberties Union of Northern California, Inc. in association with Red Dot Interactive, Inc., San Francisco, CA, 1992.

This educational interactive software program is designed to be fun for middle and high school students, identifying the boundaries and issues of freedom of expression and censorship most likely to be of concern to the student population: student journalism, campus-organizing, race relations, music, religion, and fashion. Video animation is effectively combined with music, graphics, and text in a menu-driven Macintosh Hypercard software program (requiring HyperCard 2.1, System 6.05 or greater, and a MacPlus or equivalent computer). The "Profiles" menu features eleven contemporary and historical figures significant to the establishment of First Amendment rights, including Emma Goldman, the Iroquois Confederacy, Dolores Huerta, Malcolm X, Robert Mapplethorpe, and 2 Live Crew. Highly recommended. Available free of cost to students, teachers, parents, and educators from the Northern California ACLU, 1663 Mission Street, Suite 460, San Francisco, CA 94103.

Hentoff, Nat. ***The First Freedom: A Tumultuous History of Free Speech in America***. New York: Delacorte Press, 1980.

Chapters such as "Students/Teachers/Librarians: Free-speaking 'Persons' under the Constitution" and "The Hard, Early Times of the First Amendment from the Alien and Sedition Acts of 1798 to the 'Red Scare' of the First World War" provide an introduction for high school students to the issues and principles involved in the fight for free speech. Excellent discussions of real court cases presented in an interesting, readable manner.

Howe, Irving. ***World of Our Fathers***. New York: Harcourt Brace Jovanovich, 1976.

Excellent reference material for the high school student about the journey of the East European Jews to America, specifically New York City, and the life they found and made. A useful companion for studying Goldman's life and for reading other novels of the period such as Cahan's ***The Rise of David Levinsky***.

Meltzer, Milton. ***Bread—and Roses: The Struggle of American Labor, 1865-1915***. New York: Alfred A. Knopf, 1967. Reprint. New York: New American Library, 1977.

Approximately 200 pages of visually appealing text, documents, photographs, and political cartoons about the rise of the unions for the advanced junior high or high school student. Includes a glossary of labor terms, bibliography, and index.

Orwell, George. ***Homage to Catalonia***. London: Secker and Warburg, 1938. Reprint. New York: Harcourt Brace and World, 1952. Reprint. New York: Harcourt Brace Jovanovich, 1980.

Orwell, the English journalist and novelist, went to report on the Spanish Civil War but ended up joining the fight against the Fascists. His account of his experiences and of the bitter divisions within the Republican ranks exposed the destructiveness of the Soviet-supported Spanish Communist party. This observation of what appeared to him totalitarianism in practice and his abhorrence of it was reflected in his later novels, *Animal Farm* (1945) and *Nineteen Eighty-Four* (1949). Although not formally part of the curriculum, Goldman's last years were devoted to the cause of the Spanish anarchists in the Spanish Civil War.

Roediger, Dave, and Franklin Rosemont, eds. ***Haymarket Scrapbook***. Chicago: Charles H. Kerr Publishing Company, 1986.

An excellent resource on the Haymarket bombing and the execution and subsequent pardon of the accused anarchists, whose cause inspired Goldman. The book includes contemporary newspaper accounts of the event and its aftermath, writings by those directly involved and others whose lives were touched by the incident, short articles by historians, and numerous illustrations.

Schlissel, Lillian, ed. ***The World of Randolph Bourne***. New York: E. P. Dutton, 1965.

This is an important anthology of writings by a critic who vigorously opposed U.S. participation in World War I. Part III presents other writers' contrasting opinions of the war; part IV features Bourne's essays on the war. Students should also read his essay, "The State." For advanced high school students only.

Stein, Leon. ***The Triangle Fire***. Philadelphia: J. B. Lippincott, 1962. Reprint. New York: Carroll & Graf, 1985.

The definitive study of the tragic fire at the Triangle Shirtwaist Company in New York City that resulted in the deaths of 146 workers, most of them young women. Appropriate for high school students.

Vigilante, David. ***The Constitution in Crisis: The Red Scare of 1919-1920***. Los Angeles: National Center for History in the Schools, University of California, Los Angeles, 1991.

This study unit for grades 9-12 includes teacher background materials, three lesson plans—"The Law," "The Case against the Reds," and "The Courage of Their Convictions"—and student handouts of original documents on this dramatic event in modern American history.

Werstein, Irving. ***Strangled Voices: The Story of the Haymarket Affair***. New York: Macmillan, 1969.

Approximately 100 pages about the Haymarket tragedy with illustrations of the events and documents. Appropriate for junior high and high school students. An interesting, well-written introduction to a critical episode in late nineteenth-century U.S. history.

Zinn, Howard. ***A People's History of the United States***. New York: Harper & Row Publishers, 1980.

A popular text for its recounting of episodes in history frequently ignored in standard texts, this book tells, as Zinn describes, "a history disrespectful of governments and respectful of people's movements of resistance." The book begins with an account of "Columbus, the Indians, and Human Progress," and ends with a reflection on the prospect of "a population united for fundamental change." Of particular relevance for students eager to learn more about the life and times of Emma Goldman are chapter 12, "The Empire and the People," chapter 13, "The Socialist Challenge," and chapter 14, "War Is the Health of the State."

WOMEN'S HISTORY

Baum, Charlotte, Paula Hyman, and Sonya Michel. ***The Jewish Woman in America***. New York: Dial Press, 1976. Reprint. New York: New American Library, 1977.

An excellent account of the varying experiences of Jewish women in America, from the first small Sephardic migration through the Reform movement that flourished among the early German immigrants, to the later mass immigration of Eastern European Jews in the late nineteenth and early twentieth centuries and accompanying union and Bund activity. Henrietta Szold, Emma Lazarus, Rose Schneiderman, and others appear in this rich history of women presented through biography, memoirs, and oral history.

Berkin, Carol Ruth, and Mary Beth Norton. ***Women of America: A History***. Boston: Houghton Mifflin, 1979.

Essays in this book focus on women's experience in America and provide excellent primary source documents. Included is information on feminist Charlotte Perkins Gilman, Irish immigrant women in upstate New York, Chinese immigrant women in nineteenth-century California, and the planned parenthood movement.

Evans, Sara M. ***Born for Liberty: A History of Women in America***. New York: Free Press, 1989.

One of the best one-volume surveys of American women's history published to date, this book discusses Goldman and her role in securing women's rights in the chapter titled "Women and Modernity," an in-depth look at women's issues and activism in the early 1900s. A good reference for high school students.

Glenn, Susan A. ***Daughters of the Shtetl: Life and Labor in the Immigrant Generation***. Ithaca, N.Y.: Cornell University Press, 1990.

This book for the advanced high school reader examines the experiences of young Jewish immigrant women in the garment industry, showing the contrast between their lives in the small, tradition-bound Jewish towns of Eastern Europe (the *shtetls*) and the greater degree of independence they experienced through the world of work, trade unions, and leisure in the United States.

Kerber, Linda K., and Jane Sherron De Hart, eds. ***Women's America: Refocusing the Past.*** 3d ed. New York: Oxford University Press, 1991.

This comprehensive sampling of documents and articles in the field of American women's history provides a theoretical framework for examining how reproduction, economics, politics, and changing ideologies have interacted since the colonial period.

Kessler-Harris, Alice. ***Out to Work: A History of Wage-earning Women in the United States***. New York: Oxford University Press, 1982.

A history of working women from colonial times to the present suitable for advanced high school students. Goldman is mentioned in relation to women's persistent attempts to achieve both sexual and economic independence.

Lerner, Gerda, ed. ***The Female Experience: An American Documentary***. Indianapolis: Bobbs-Merrill, 1977.

These primary sources from the colonial period through the 1970s document issues of prevailing importance to women. Particularly relevant to this unit are the sections on women in industrial employment, organizing women workers, women in politics, and a woman's right to control her own body.

O'Neill, William. ***Everyone Was Brave: The Rise and Fall of Feminism in America.*** Chicago: Quadrangle Books, 1969.

Approximately 350-page history of feminism in America from Victorian times through the 1960s. Some leading feminists, including Goldman, are not mentioned, but this remains a good reference for analysis of social institutions like the family, the school, and the church and the effects of their policies on women.

Papachristou, Judith. ***Women Together: A History in Documents of the Women's Movement in the United States.*** New York: Alfred A. Knopf, 1976.

A collection of important documents tracking the women's movement in the United States from the 1830s through its resurgence in the 1970s. Included are speeches, reports, supportive and critical newspaper accounts, court trials, manifestos, and first-person accounts.

Sanders, Beverly. ***Women in the Progressive Era: 1890-1920.*** (Women in American History Series.) Boston: Education Development Center, 1979.

This booklet is one in a series of four that narrate women's lives and accomplishments during particular periods of American history. Written for the secondary level student, the resource contains inquiry questions and activities and includes a chapter on women's contributions to arts and letters.

Wertheimer, Barbara Mayer. ***We Were There: The Story of Working Women in America.*** New York: Pantheon Books, 1977.

Focusing on the role of women as workers through American history, this book offers richly detailed information on the wage-earning woman from 1886 to 1910 and on the participation of women in the emerging trade unions between 1900 and 1914.

With Speech as My Weapon: Emma Goldman and the First Ammendment

A Unit of Study for Grades 8-12

by
Candace Falk, Stephen Cole, and Sally Thomas
The Emma Goldman Papers Project
University of California, Berkeley

NATIONAL CENTER FOR HISTORY IN THE SCHOOLS
University of California, Los Angeles

The Emma Goldman Papers

A site on the World Wide Web

http://sunsite.berkeley.edu/Goldman/

Berkeley Digital Library SunSITE

What

The Emma Goldman Papers are an online presentation of historical documents and scholarly resources that reflect on the life and influence of Emma Goldman (1869-1940), the Russian-born anarchist and life-long advocate of women's rights, freedom of expression, and social justice. The collection is a unique and dynamic representation of Goldman's dialogue with many of the leading political theorists, writers, journalists, and creative thinkers on the burning issues of her time --- strategies for winning rights for workers, birth control and women's independence, the failures of the Russian Revolution, and the social significance of the modern drama, among others.

The site also offers extensive excerpts from the award-winning reference *Emma Goldman: A guide to Her Life and Documentary Sources*, including the complete indexes of correspondence, government documents, and Goldman's writings; and a detailed chronology and biographical and bibliographical essays by the editors of the Emma Goldman Papers Project. The web site includes samples from the massive collection of Goldman's papers published as *The Emma Goldman Papers: A Microfilm Edition* (69 reels). Additional material is added regularly.

Why

The Digital library features a rich collection of material that will interest anyone engaged in research and reflection on the ideas and individuals that shaped America. Goldman's life and thoughts offer insight into our diverse heritage and an appreciation of the struggles that were waged to advance social justice. Digital reproductions of documents simulate the thrilling experience of viewing archival manuscripts and offer an unfiltered opportunity to learn about Goldman through her own words.

Highlights

- Digital reproductions of original letters and lecture bills, including correspondence with novelist Theodore Dreiser and journalist George Seldes --- Material that first appeared in *The Emma Goldman Papers: A Microfilm Edition* (Chadwyck-Healey, 1991).
- Photographs of Goldman and her associates (from the Library of Congress).
- Electronic texts of selections from Goldman's published writings, including *Anarchism and Other Essays* (1910).
- Extensive excerpts from *Emma Goldman: A Guide to Her Life and Documentary Sources* (Chadwyck-Healey, 1995).
- The full text and illustrations from the Emma Goldman Papers travelling Exhibition.
- transcribed and annotated documents from the *Emma Goldman Papers,* book edition (University of California Press, forthcoming).
- The Life and Times of Emma Goldman: A Curriculum for Middle and High School Students (UC Regents, 1992), presenting the themes of immigration, freedom of expression, women's rights, anti-militarism, and the art and literature of social change.

Evaluation of
The Life and Times of Emma Goldman Curriculum

1. Did you know about Goldman's life and work before using this guide?

2. Which documents did you find most appropriate for classroom use? Why?

3. Which documents did you find inappropriate for classroom use? Why?

4. Does the material seem age- and skill-appropriate for your students?

5. Were the document questions and activity suggestions helpful?

6. Do you have any suggestions for improving these materials?

Name of school/location: ____

Class level you teach: ____________________ Public/Private School?: __________

How did you learn about the curriculum?____________________________________

Send us your name and address if you would like to be on our mailing list.

We appreciate your feedback! *Please mail to:*
The Emma Goldman Papers, U.C. Berkeley, 2372 Ellsworth Street, Berkeley, CA 94720.